The Carnival of Animals
A Tale of Many Tails

The Carnival of Animals
A Tale of Many Tails

by

Robert L. and Fran Williams Smith

CREATIVE ARTS BOOK COMPANY
Berkeley, California

The Carnival of Animals is published by Donald S. Ellis
and distributed by Creative Arts Book Company

For information contact:
Creative Arts Book Company
833 Bancroft Way
Berkeley, California 94710
1-800-848-7789

ISBN 0-88739-410-8
Library of Congress Catalog Number 2001097071

Stories

Dedication

The Carnival of Animals is dedicated to our many animal friends who have lived with us for a half century. It is a love story that reminds us of how important their time with us is, and has been. They have offered companionship, amusement, and entertainment, and they have offered friendship and unquestioned love, openly and without reservation. They have enriched our lives, something for which we are eternally grateful.

The Carnival of Animals
A Tale of Many Tails

The Carnival of Animals

This is a tale of many tails. It is about cats, dogs, raccoons, and other creatures that have graced our home and garden over the past fifty years. It is about the joys our animal friends have generated with their presence, and it is about how they have enriched our lives with their acquaintance, no matter how brief their visit. Some of our animal friends have been members of the family and others only passing acquaintances. But, each new occasion that arises reminds us of the pleasures and happiness our animal friends bring to us, and we welcome the new additions to the family as another "about to be" old friend.

What we have set out to share is not a narrative with a plot; rather, it is an eclectic recounting of personal experiences with animals we will never forget, a virtual carnival of animals. Regardless of whether they were/are members of the household, visitors, or part of the outdoor wildlife, the ensuing tales are about "friends" that were/are a part of family life at our house on the hill.

+++

As children both my wife and I had pets, but they were generally shared with other family members. They really weren't our special friends. My wife's first dog was Ruff, a wire hair fox terrier who really was her father's dog, but was trained, fed, and groomed by her mother. My wife's memories of Ruff were generally associated with what they did with the dog. She was an observer with a part-time, but important, relationship.

The one major exception occurred when she was living in Culver City in Southern California. The town was the home of Metro Golden Mayer, the world's largest movie studio, where her father worked as a special effects man. As happens with all kids, the occasion arose where she felt that her parents were unforgivingly mean to her. She decided to teach them a lesson and run away from home. Under the close super-

Ruff

2

vision of Ruff, along to offer protection, she made her way to Venice Boulevard. There, amid traffic and bustle, she and Ruff had a serious discussion about the merits of this decision. Wisdom prevailed, and she and Ruff returned home. Both of them knew the importance of making a statement without overdoing it.

I had many cats and dogs that were my own. Most of them were short term relationships due to the way we found each other. "They followed me home," I would explain to my mother, or, "John's mother gave me the puppy because we are such good friends." Whatever the reason, these relationships were of limited duration until Pal and I joined forces against the world of powerful adults. I was ten, and he was just a pup.

Pal was a gift from an uncle whose bitch had just delivered him with a litter of puppies. He was a fine example of the "all dog" breed, a bit of this and that without any clearly distinguishing characteristics. From the beginning, we belonged to each other and were immediately joined in friendship. He was small, less than fifteen inches at the shoulders, and brown,

3

Pal

black, and tan with a pure white chest. To my eyes he was the handsomest dog I had ever seen. We ate together, slept together, and struggled together against the frightening world of adults. There was nothing I could not tell Pal, and he would listen, carefully, thoughtfully, and sympathetically. He looked after me for the better part of eight years, before he was lost in what I believed to be the world's worst tragedy. My family had moved to Arizona to work in the copper mines for a brief time. In less than a year we returned to California. It was on the return that the tragedy struck. We drove back to California, but Pal had to be shipped home by railroad. During his journey home he escaped in a small town in New Mexico. Pal never arrived back in California, but a look-alike replacement did. The innocent stranger the railroad people had captured arrived in good condition, but thoroughly confused by his relocation. We were never able to convince the railroad folks that he was not Pal, since he did look so similar to my buddy. They insisted that the dog they had captured after Pal's escape was my dog, and no amount of protest would convince them otherwise. Hopefully they finally figured it out and returned this nice dog to his place of capture back in New Mexico.

4

Sadly, I never saw Pal again and experienced that heavy sorrow that comes from the loss of a close and valued friend. The sadness was somewhat eased by memories of our going fishing in the early hours of the morning, sharing homemade sandwiches and stolen cookies, and, the companionship of just the two of us delivering papers early each morning, often being chased by large angry dogs. No one knew the full range of the adventures we shared except Pal and me. It was always our secret since our activities were often ones that my parents would not have approved. Some of the best of the memories included things that could not be shared with adults who would not understand, warm summer afternoons spent together stretched out on the grass in the front yard, discussing the world, our adventures, the unfairness of adults, and all of the tomorrow's we planned to have together when we grew up. We had our share of good times, and, although fewer than they might have been, there were enough to last me a lifetime, ones rich in memories of my closest friend and buddy, Pal.

+++

The intervening years between youth and adulthood did not permit my wife or me to have animal friends. She was busy going to school, and I was temporarily interrupting my life with the experience of war, and later, with obtaining the education I had ignored in my earlier years.

Although my future wife and I had known each other at junior college, it was not until we both attended the University of California at Santa Barbara, after World War II, that we began seriously dating. We became friends, fell in love, and married in 1950. The following year I accepted employment with a state correctional agency in San Francisco, and we moved to Berkeley, just across the bay.

+++

Our first apartment was in a basement in a house about midway up in the Berkeley hills. The views from the living room and the bedroom were spectacular, and we became committed to having a view of the San Francisco

Bay wherever we eventually owned our own home. In those days, my pay as a trainee was one hundred thirty dollars per month. With my educational benefits as a veteran, my income was a little over two hundred dollars per month. My wife had to work for us to survive so she became a social worker in a nearby county.

The apartment landlord owned two cats, Nikki and Chino. They came with the apartment—at least they behaved as if they did. Chino was, fat, long-haired, black, and loved to sleep in the bedroom facing the bay. The room was generally sunny and warm, and Chino thought it belonged to him. Nikki was a light gray, short hair tabby who was a natural born hustler. He had learned to sit up and beg for food, something that he did without our encouragement. His private place was on top of the refrigerator—an old relic with a coil on top that generated heat. Both of them waited for us to come home in the evening and then moved in for the night. It was our first experience with "loaner cats," animals belonging to someone else, but acting like they belong to you. Nikki became a real attachment, and our landlords were almost ready to give him to us for our new house when we moved out. They reconsidered, however, and Nikki remained to charm the next people who rented the basement apartment.

+++

Our early days in Berkeley were exciting and stimulating. New ideas were in vogue in both of our chosen fields of employment. I was working as a trainee in corrections, and my wife was working as a social worker in a new program for the learning disabled. Berkeley was a fun place to live, offering many opportunities for culture, the arts, and pleasant living. The university was still a place where students were taught by their professors and not teaching assistants, where classes were small enough to provide individual attention. It was not the ever expanding behemoth it is now. I worked full time and went to graduate school while Fran supported and encouraged me.

We had little money, but what we did make we saved. By 1953, we began to think that it might be possible for us to buy our own home. We house shopped as most young people do, looking at places we could not afford, and dreamed. We planned and struggled to think of ways we could accumulate the down payment for a home. Then, one afternoon, we read a description in the newspaper that sounded like our impossible dream; "Small comfortable two bedroom home in the Berkeley Hills with fireplace, view of the Bay—priced to sell." We made an appointment and went out that evening to see "our dream house." It was, in reality, an unlandscaped barren, cracker box, but it did have a fireplace. Sitting near the crest of a large hill, at an altitude of almost 1,000 feet, it also had the required panoramic view of the bay. Surrounded by trees, and with a regional park only minutes away, we felt we had found our house. The reasonable asking price, however, represented a figure that we could barely imagine or consider. By today's standards, the price would be regarded as chicken feed, but then, to us, it was a fortune beyond counting. Even if we could somehow manage the down payment, how could we make the monthly payments that would go on for years? In a blind act of youthful faith, we committed ourselves to the purchase. Then, for the next three weeks, we both suffered anxiety attacks about our impulsive action. How were we ever going to survive the decision, or as we felt at the time, the serious mistake.

Even with both of us working, our income did not seem to support so grand a purchase. Yet, we managed. We secured a California veteran's loan, and within two months moved into our castle—a cracker box without furniture or appliances. But, the house is not the story, only the setting for the loving experiences with our animal carnival.

+++

We were in our house for only a few months when one of Fran's coworkers asked for help with a problem. Her female cat had gotten out when in heat and was now in a family way. She desperately needed to place her errant cat's progeny. We made no commitments, but did agree to consider the matter once the kittens were born and ready for adoption. The litter was adorable. Mostly black, one of the kittens had white paws and a white front that made him look like he was wearing a tuxedo. He was funny, cuddly, loving, and all of the other things that make kittens so adorable. We watched the litter play, tumbling and falling all over one another before we acknowledged the choice that we had made the minute we walked into the door. The tuxedo kid would go home with the Smiths.

Even though we had made our choice on the first visit, it would still be several weeks before Nibs, our cat's new name, could come home with us. In the meantime, my wife's friend called to tell us she had placed all of the kittens except one. The people who had selected her decided at the last minute not to take her home. She asked my wife for help once again in placing the remaining kitten. Of course, that meant we had to see it before we could make any recommenda-tions regarding possible placement—-a traditional mis-take we make regularly. We went back to see the kit-ten. Jet black, she attacked the other kittens, forcing them to play. She batted shoe laces, mostly mine, looked wide eyed and purred, and did all of the other things that kittens do to get into your heart. Before we left, the kitten was placed. She would come home with Nibs when they were ready. Thus begins the epoch of Nibs and Grundoone, our first two animal friends. The carnival had begun.

Nibs and Grundoone

Nibs and Grundoone were members of our family for the next fourteen years. They brightened our lives with their adventures and misadventures. Not alone during this period, they shared their space with the wild critters that roamed our garden almost every night. There was Bungee, Georgeena, and the Little Gentleman, members of a fat-tailed raccoon family. Then there was Spread Eagle, a member of the long thin-tailed raccoon family who also lived on the hill and regularly spent his evenings partying in the garden. In turn, the raccoons shared their part of the garden with the salamanders; Inky, the cat from next door; Curly the dog; and later, Rags and Katy.

+++

Nibs and Grundoone were only six weeks old when

we brought them home. Being litter mates, they were always together getting into trouble, snoozing, playing, and enjoying their new world of exploration. In addition to their own back yard, the kittens had a whole unexplored world around them filled with strange creatures. Next-door was a great open lot that stretched clear up to Grizzly Peak Boulevard. Eucalyptus trees were everywhere. There were gophers, moles, field mice, and small grass snakes that made every day an adventure for our two friends. The hill was alive with birds, squirrels, deer, and the ever present raccoons. It was a place of wonder for two small kittens.

Curly was their first encounter with a dog. He was a great brown airedale and lived up the hill in back of our house. He was also the only dog that we ever knew who smiled when he greeted us. I know that the skeptics among you will insist that this was only a reflex curl of the lip, but whatever it was, he always did it when approaching us. He would come running down the hill with his short stub of a tail, moving his whole rear end from one side to the other with a silly smile on his lips.

14

Curly

His first meeting with the kittens was something to behold. A gentle animal, friendly to man and beast alike, he came running down to greet the two new arrivals who had just ventured into the back yard. The two small kittens suddenly exploded into two great furry balls, spitting and strutting as if they could defend themselves against anything, including this silly smiling dog. Curly was stunned by the frightening demonstration and wasn't sure what was expected of him. He was discrete and sniffed from a distance before slowly retreating back up the hill, but clearly, his feelings had been hurt by these two unfriendly felines. Within a few days Curly was a fixture around the house. He served at the pleasure of the kittens as a doormat for indoor games, and an object of attack for outside sports. He patiently ignored the frenzy of the kittens who insisted on running over and around him as he tried valiantly to snooze in the late afternoon sun. Later, the kittens could be found curled up with their new friend, sharing the wonderful comfort of the warm sun.

+++

Contrary to what some have told me, animals do have distinct personalities. Even a casual observation can affirm this. Nibs and Grundoone were as different as day and night. Their behavior and response to reprimands were clear indications of their basic differences in dealing with people. Nibs learned slowly, but he had one of the largest superegos we had ever encountered. If you yelled at him for some indiscretion or misadventure, he would slink, hide, and exhibit every characteristic of a severely abused animal. He was completely shattered by unfriendly behavior or sounds in humans. Grundoone, on the other hand, was a perfect example of a sociopath. She knew right from wrong and could not care less. If there was someone in a crowd who could not stand cats, she would seek them out and make them suffer. On more than one occasion she was thrown across the room by an unsuspecting visitor who did not expect to have a cat in his or her lap. Such rejection would have crushed Nibs, but not Grundoone. She would turn her flying body, land gently on all fours, and with complete aplomb, walk gracefully away from the offended party. She was also the

16

Grundoone

adventurer. She would climb the highest trees, encourage Nibs to join her, and then abandon him until someone came to his rescue. Nibs stumbled into catching local game on rare occasions. She was the huntress, and frighteningly successful in her pursuits. One craved affection, the other took it at her leisure and under her conditions.

Grundoone was also one of two "hiders" who have lived with us. She loved to hide when we were trying to get ready to leave the house and either wanted to put her out, or on occasion be sure she was in. She sensed these times and would disappear. The first time it happened, we were going out for the evening and didn't want to leave her locked in. We had fed her and knew she was in, but when it came time to leave, we could not find her. We looked everywhere, in closets, under beds, chairs, and tables. By any reasonable assessment, Grundoone was not in the house. We were wrong; when we returned home she was waiting to greet us at the front door. She also gave us the devil for leaving her locked in. This happened several times before we finally figured out where her hiding place was.

17

Grundoone: the
disappearing cat

18

Nibs and Grundoone

We had some dark walnut bookshelves at one end of the living room. They held books, sculpture, and vases. Filled to overflowing, it never occurred to us to think of looking there for our missing cat. But, one weekend we were planning to be gone for a couple of days, and it was essential that we be sure she was out of the house. We began our search and failed once again to locate the hiding cat. Again, we covered every inch of our small home without finding any sign of her. In desperation, I got a flashlight and began a final search. Just as I was about to again admit defeat, my light caught two bright eyes looking down at me from the top of the bookshelf. She was hiding behind a large travel book that shielded her from view except for the glowing eyes. I cannot give any assurance that this was her only hiding place in the house, but from that time on it was the first location we searched when missing Ms. Grundoone.

When we were going to be away for the weekend, or even out for the evening, we frequently put Nibs and Grundoone in the basement. It was a large unfinished area with nothing in it except the furnace. Completely uncluttered there was absolutely no place to hide, yet Grundoone managed.

After being away from home one night, I went down to the basement the next morning to open the door to let our two friends out. Nibs strolled out, letting me know that it was about time, but there was no Grundoone. I turned on the light, searched the entire basement, but no cat. I thought, "there must be some way for her to get out, and I'll check tomorrow." The next day I went down to make my search. Waiting at the door was Ms. G. She strolled out as if she didn't have a care in the world. Thereafter she disappeared several other times, and I was unable to find our hiding cat. Again, in desperation, I decided I was going to find out where she was going. So, in the dark and on a ladder, I sat in the basement in the dark listening for the sounds of her and Nibs moving about. I located Nibs several times, but there was no sign of Ms. G. Finally after about an hour I heard a noise near the roof and just beyond the entry door. I flashed my light on the area, and there were two bright yellow eyes looking back at me. She had discovered that between the floor joists on the supporting wall going out to the carport, there was a small nook that must have been warm as well as private. From then on, I knew where to search.

Nibs and Grundoone

+++

Nibs rarely caught anything. The one memorable occasion that always comes to mind is the day he brought home a large dove. How he caught it we never knew, but he brought it home to show his family. As we always do, we attempted to rescue the dove since we were frequently successful in our attempts. On this day, Nibs was very proud of his catch. Mewing and calling for recognition, he carried the great bird up the hill to avoid any sudden rushes from my wife or me. We walked up, quietly reassuring him of our pride, then both shouted as loud as we could. He dropped the dove and looked as if we had attacked him. He was shattered by our unloving and unappreciative behavior. But, that was not the final insult to confront him. The great bird, which had looked lifeless, suddenly turned over, bounced off of Nib's head and took to the air in what appeared to be a very healthy condition. Nibs spent the next two days revisiting the spot where he had dropped the bird, in hopes, we are sure, that his trophy would come back.

On one other occasion Nibs was successful in the

21

Nibs and Big Bird

hunt. He caught a mole and brought it into the living room. Moles are not easily intimidated by man or beast, and bite if given the chance. Although Nibs thought it was a wonderful place to exhibit his prize, we had different thoughts. We were not familiar with the techniques or strategies for mole catching. I got a large paper bag and broom. Armed for rescue, we approached Nibs and made friendly encouraging sounds so as not to frighten him out of catching range. We wanted to reassure him that we appreciated his trophy and his willingness to share it with us. Whether it was the friendly approach or two people with a sack and broom that confused him, he dropped his prize momentarily. In that lightning moment, my wife swept him up, threw him into a back room, closed the door and began our safari for the furry quarry.

I kept reminding my wife that moles sometimes charge when wounded, something I had learned in the military from a cartoon strip called Willie and Joe. The division of labor called for her to hold the sack—in effect, being the bag lady—while I, using my cunning and stealth, swept the vicious creature into the sack with my trusty broom. Around and around the living

22

room we went with the mole outmaneuvering us at every turn. We finally had him cornered, and with care, moved in for the capture. I swear I heard the mole growl when he charged the bag. But, we were ready for the attack. I deftly swept him into the open sack which my wife quickly closed. He was not finished, however. That little demon began clawing and ripping the sack in his desperation to escape. My wife got the sack and creature to the back door before he escaped to the ground and then retaining wall where he disappeared.

Exhausted from the chase we brought Nibs out for reassurance and some affection to show him that we appreciated his marvelous hunting efforts. People often are good actors when dealing with their animal's indiscretions. After a couple of glasses of wine, our perspectives improved, and we toasted the mole that got away.

+++

Grundoone was something else. It took only one encounter for her to recognize that people could not be trusted with captured prizes, particularly field mice.

23

Attack of the mole

She always wanted us to see her trophies, but only from a distance. Being only half of Nib's seventeen pounds, she was fast and agile. That meant that field mice and gophers were a steady part of her diet. She was a natural huntress. Of all of her shared catches, the small grass snakes were the least acceptable. She never killed them, but did enjoy playing with them. It was not unusual to find one on the deck or in the kitchen where she had become bored and left us a present. We became very skilled with the broom and sack routine initially developed for the mole.

The success of either cat in hunting always was a surprise to us. Someone had told us early on that garlic was good for cats and kept them from getting worms. Based on this advice we initiated a diet for the cats laced with garlic powder. They got large doses of it on anything we fed them. You knew it when either one entered a room, particularly if you were down wind. With a strong and pure garlic breath we always wondered how they got close enough to anything to catch.

Nibs and Grundoone

+++

As different as Nibs and Grundoone were, they were inseparable companions. Wherever one was, the other was never far behind. The vacant lot next door, always a forest of weeds in the spring, offered unlimited adventure and excitement for our two friends. They would begin at different ends of the lot and slowly slink their way toward one another in an effort to ambush the other. We would spend hours on our deck watching their antics unfold in the swaying grass and weeds, always ending in a furry explosion of excitement when they charged one another. Occasionally Curly would join in the game, but he was really not expected to be a participant since he gave away the action long before Nibs and Grundoone found one another. They loved the lot and seemed resentful when, late in summer, the fire department came by to burn the tall grass as a part of the city fire suppression program. Yet even that event gave rise to new opportunities for the two friends. What had been grass and weed cover now became open ground where gopher and mole holes were clearly visible, thereby providing new games to test Nibs and Grundoone's hunting skills. As

the years passed, many things changed, but not their
constant companionship.

+++

Several years into our association, Nibs disappeared for two weeks. We looked all over our property,
advertised, scoured the neighborhood, but to no avail.
We grieved and were finally coming to terms with our
loss. I was working in the back yard, when I heard
what seemed to be a familiar yowl. Down the hill came
a now scrawny, black and white cat telling me about
his adventures. Nibs was severely dehydrated and had
lost a great deal of weight, but otherwise, appeared to
be in good condition. Halfway down the hill,
Grundoone appeared from nowhere and ran past me to
greet her errant companion. Initially the greeting was
friendly, with much rubbing and meowing, then, as if
she remembered the pain of his absence, hissed and
cuffed him about the ears before turning her back and
disappearing into the vacant lot next door. As was cus-
tomary with Nibs, he looked shocked and hurt by the
hostility shown by his sister. I picked him up and tried
to offer some reassurance, but at the moment, he just

wanted food and water, and had no time for any emotional nonsense.

We never did find out what happened, but assumed that a neighbor had gone on vacation and unknowingly locked our friend in a garage, house, or basement. Nibs loved people and had felt free to sneak into their house for refreshment and rest without invitation. He stayed close to our house after that, and seemed to have gained control over his need to roam the wilds of the Berkeley hills.

+++

Over the years, both Nibs and Grundoone had adventures, but never equally. Nibs was incident-prone; things were always just happening to him. Grundoone quickly learned which end of a skunk is dangerous and avoided it at all cost. Nibs never did. In the midst of our carnival of animals, the old boy would sit with raccoons and skunks with complete indifference. As a result he often came in with something more than a faint scent of skunk. I came to feel that Nibs identified with the skunks black and white coloring

27

Getting Skunked

and lovely bushy tails. He seemed to see them as some form of distant relative—or at least he did until one evening he obviously made a serious mistake and got the full effect of an unhappy skunk.

I came into the kitchen to get a glass of water, but was immediately distracted by a strong skunk scent. I went to the backdoor to identify the culprit. There sat Nibs. I yelled for Fran. She joined me reluctantly since the old boy really was quite gamey. We busily discussed options. It was late, no vet was available for information about descenting a cat. Both of us remembered something about tomato juice being good for dealing with such situations. I searched madly for tomato juice. I failed, but did locate some cans of V8 Juice. My wife and I put on rubber gloves, so all we had to do now was snatch Nibs up, dunk him in V8 Juice, and hope for the best.

By the time we were ready Nibs had tired of licking himself, particularly since he registered distaste with every lick. I opened the door and gained the full benefit of his having been sprayed. I clutched him with my rubber gloves and quickly moved him to the sink where my wife had prepared a large bowl with two cans of V8 Juice. Everything went fine until his feet touched the liquid. He squirmed and tried every move he had to get out of my clutch, but down in the juice he went, not without splashing both of us. My wife poured cup after cup over his shoulders and down his back in spite of his desperate struggle to escape. Nibs began to yowl great cries for rescue. Grundoone showed up to offer help, but was not sure that the wet, red cat was known to her. Finally, Nibs calmed down and accepted his fate, but reluctantly.

We bathed him fore and aft, top to bottom, and although initially it did not seem to make much difference the scent eventually became less intense. After full immersion in the vegetable juice, we moved him to warm suds. Pacified, our roaring tom was forlorn but no longer resisting our handling. It wasn't till we got to the rubdown with towels that he decided things were not as bad as he had thought. He actually seemed to enjoy the rubbing. Finally, we had done all we could think of when my wife thought of shaving lotion. She suggested I try a dash on him to tame the last whiffs of skunk. I did, and Nibs jumped down and ran out to the living room as if I had committed some cardinal sin. He licked and groomed himself with intensity for the next thirty minutes. Just before departing for the bedroom, Grundoone came over to inspect him. She came within about twelve inches, sniffed, hissed, and backed off.

The house was thoroughly aired for two days before the final traces of the encounter began to disappear. During the next two weeks, at the slightest suggestion of a suspicious smell my wife and I would grab Nibs and give him a sniff, only to discover that he still smelled like shaving lotion.

Any reasonable animal would have learned from this experience, but three nights later Nibs was sitting in the garden with his skunk friends as if nothing had ever happened.

+++

When we first moved into the house on the hill, before Nibs and Grundoone's arrival, the yard was not landscaped, and we faced open uncovered areas without vegetation of any kind. Garden areas were at best

30

only suggestions set off by old railroad ties used as retaining walls. The main wall was four to five feet back from the rear of the house, four feet tall, and about forty feet in length. Old and rotting when the ties were set, there were already breeches that let dirt encroach on the back of the house and the walk area that separated the house from the retaining wall.

We both worked full-time and recognized that to replace the rotting retaining wall would take considerable time and money, neither of which we had much of. Whatever was done, we would have to do after work and on weekends and holidays. At best, it would take us several months to pull out the old railroad ties, get rid of them, and replace them with whatever we could afford.

We began the project with the enthusiasm of youth and completed it many months later with new-found experience, and gratitude for the health, strength and energy of our youth. First, we pulled out the dirt and railroad ties. We cut the ties into smaller pieces that could be lifted. The cutting was done by hand since we could not afford a chain saw. The work was done a few

SOUTH PARK
DRIVE
CLOSED
TO SAVE THE
NEWTS

feet at a time whenever we had an extra minute. When enough pieces of the ties had been cut and collected, we burned them on the lot next door. It was a dirty, tedious job that fascinated Nibs and Grundoone. Every excavation produced new evidence of moles and gophers. The animals were always with us in our labors, optimistically looking for unearned prizes. One night, I found to my surprise, salamanders or newts as they are sometimes called.

I am not a salamander fancier, but my wife is. I do not really appreciate any of God's creatures that squirm or slink, and look wet and slippery. In taking the railroad ties apart, I discovered pocket after pocket of these slippery little beasts. There was no argument over the division of labor. My wife could, without any objections on my part, take care of relocating the salamanders. Nibs and Grundoone were fascinated with the new discovery, but unlike other new experiences, had sense enough to not get involved.

Over the next year, I would dig out a tie, scream for help when I discovered a salamander pocket, and my wife would come out to relocate them somewhere else

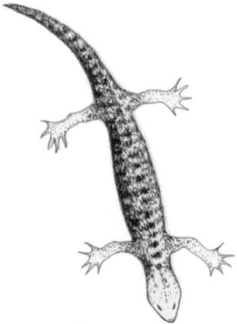

32

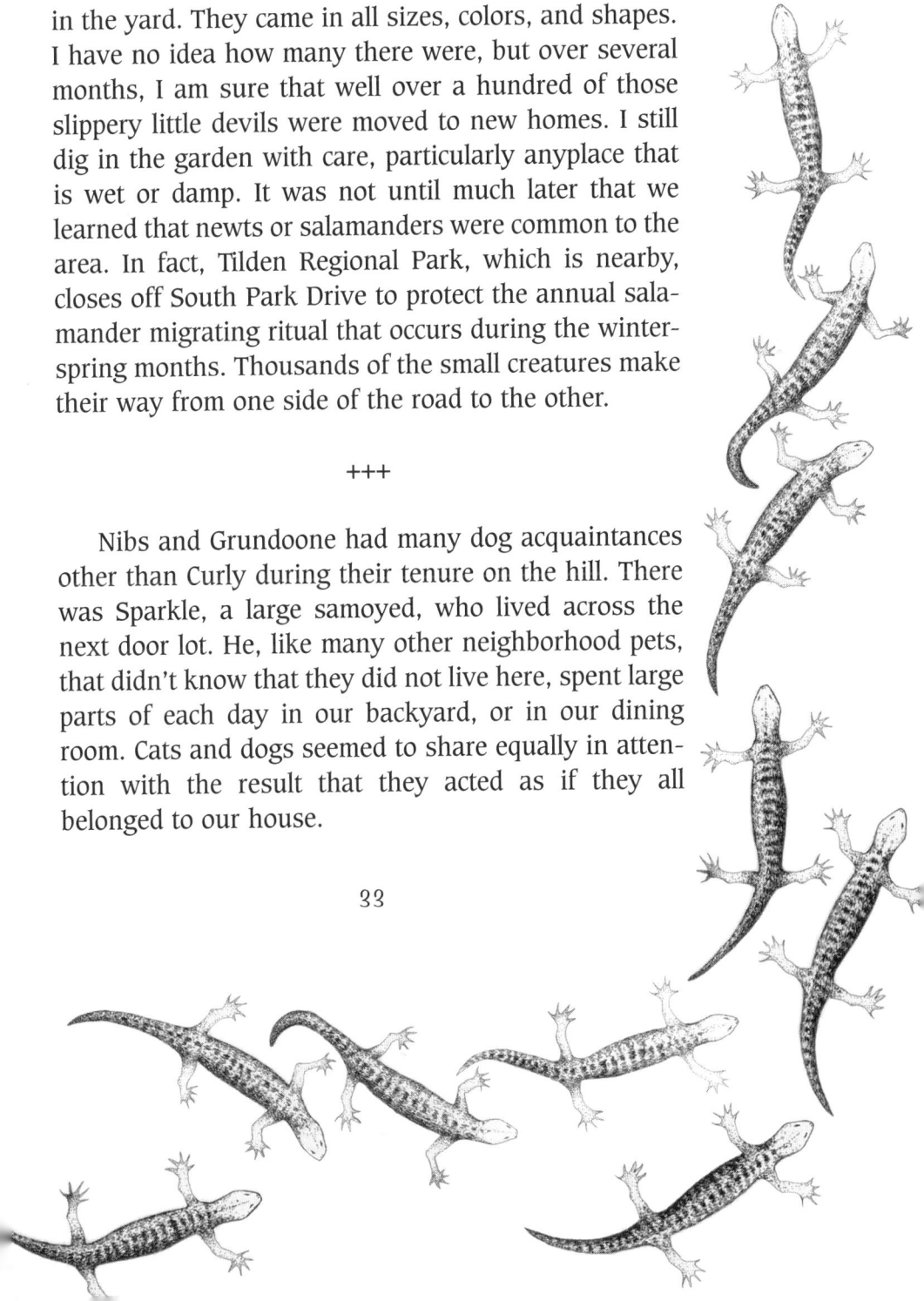

in the yard. They came in all sizes, colors, and shapes. I have no idea how many there were, but over several months, I am sure that well over a hundred of those slippery little devils were moved to new homes. I still dig in the garden with care, particularly anyplace that is wet or damp. It was not until much later that we learned that newts or salamanders were common to the area. In fact, Tilden Regional Park, which is nearby, closes off South Park Drive to protect the annual sala-mander migrating ritual that occurs during the winter-spring months. Thousands of the small creatures make their way from one side of the road to the other.

+++

Nibs and Grundoone had many dog acquaintances other than Curly during their tenure on the hill. There was Sparkle, a large samoyed, who lived across the next door lot. He, like many other neighborhood pets, that didn't know that they did not live here, spent large parts of each day in our backyard, or in our dining room. Cats and dogs seemed to share equally in atten-tion with the result that they acted as if they all belonged to our house.

33

Rags and Katy were of a slightly different genera, however. They belonged to the neighbors living two houses to the north. Rags was the first to introduce himself. He was a great shaggy sheep dog that never seemed to be groomed or dry. In the midst of any rainy day we could count on Rags to appear at the back door wet, looking forlorn and hungry. He would eat anything and showed it. Bread, bones, vegetables, whatever, Rags was not one to ignore anything that could be eaten or buried for later use. He showed up regularly at the dinner hour and peered into the dining room through the open French doors. He would just stand in his sorrowful way and wait, and wait, and wait until we broke down and gave him a treat.

Katy succeeded Rags some years later. She was much more direct in her approach. Her arrival at the French doors was always announced by baying sounds that beagles make. They were not just barks, but a whole litany of howls, yelps, and moans that would wake the dead. She, too, was less than careful about her diet as her round belly testified. Both of these neighborhood animal friends were a part of the early Nibs and Grundoone period. They, just like

Curly, became fixtures around which our cats learned to navigate without incident.

+++

My wife's parents were visiting when one of the many raccoon families living on the hill stopped by the back door to investigate what was going on. Fran's father had never seen a raccoon and was fascinated by the little critters. He grabbed virtually everything in the kitchen he could find to feed them, including a bag of Mother's Oatmeal Cookies and raw eggs. That established a precedent. From that time on, we regularly bought packages of five dozen Mother's Oatmeal Cookies to keep on hand for the raccoons. Raw eggs were reserved for pregnant raccoons or those really tenacious at begging. After a few months of this my wife realized that we were engaging in a very expensive activity. In the spirit of economy, she decided that she would bake cookies rather than purchase them. In addition, and in the interest of the raccoons' health, she decided to cut the sugar content substantially.

RUTH'S OATMEAL COOKIES

SUGAR FREE

Handbaked with tender, loving care Using only the finest ingredients.

MOTHER'S OATMEAL COOKIES

IN TESTS PREFERRED BY 10 OUT OF 10 RACOONS

I have never known my wife to bake anything, and, to say the least, I was surprised when one evening I came home to the wonderful smell of fresh cookies baking. Anxious to test her creativity she thrust a cookie out and said, "Try it." I did and thought they tasted good, particularly for a first effort. She could hardly wait for her furry friends to arrive so that she could try the results of her baking talents on them. In the interim, I enjoyed several more cookies. She gathered a pile of cookies for the first bandit who was already waiting at the door. Excitedly, she offered him a fresh home baked cookie which he eagerly accepted. He carefully sniffed it, handled it in his paws, sniffed it once again, and dropped it. He came back for another, repeated the same operation and again rejected it before returning to the door for the real thing. Out of curiosity, I went to the cupboard and got one of Mother's Oatmeal Cookies, prepared by the loving hands of Nabisco. I gave the cookie to my wife who, in turn, gave it to the raccoon. He snatched it from her hand, wolfed it down, and returned for another and another before she offered him one of her homemade cookies. I hate to report that the homemade cookies failed ten out of ten tests. The raccoons wanted only the real thing. No amount of consolation eased my wife's broken spirit. She has not baked an oatmeal cookie since that day. Neither has she accepted my argument that raccoons are sugar freaks and addicted to experiencing sugar highs from Mother's Oatmeal Cookies.

Our local bandits came in two varieties, fat-tailed and long-tailed. Bungee was our first raccoon friend and was a member of the fat-tailed branch of the species. Bungee's name came from her many, and I do mean many, ugly wounds acquired over the years in fights. Always gentle and friendly with us, she was vicious with other raccoons. Georgeena was not a fighter, but a lover. Her name came from our discovery that she was not a he. Originally named Lonesome George, we changed it when she arrived with her litter of kittens. A third visitor was named Little Gentleman. The gentlest of the group, he was hardly little. His favorite pose was to sit on a step, let his belly hang down and, in a state of sheer ecstasy, scratch with an enthusiasm that lasted for several minutes. The fourth member of this early group was Spread Eagle. He gained his name by coming to the bricks just beyond

the French doors and spreading out on his belly with all four paws spread out before and behind in different directions. Lying in this fashion he watched the action, whatever it was, with absolute fascination. He spent whole evenings with us in this position. Often we looked out to see our cats flanked by the raccoons, all looking in the house, the cats to get in and the raccoons to get a handout.

As familiar as they became, when with family our bandit friends appeared only after hiding their kittens in the nearby brush or trees. We knew they were there because of the high-pitched chittering sounds they make while young. Whenever the mothers thought it was time, each would present her kittens to us, generally, small furry balls not much bigger than I could hold in the palm of my hand—something even we were never foolish enough to do. The kittens grew quickly, and each survivor contributed to the raccoon count visiting our house nightly. Kittens regularly returned as adults with their own offspring, something that is satisfying, but also a trial. Feeding raccoons quickly contributes to overcrowding, and the two or three original visitors become fifteen, twenty, or twenty-five in a few years. It then became necessary to manage the population by stopping the feeding and ignoring them indefinitely. This was not easy after each of us had become dependent upon the other, us for friendship, they for food.

+++

Spring meant pregnancy for the raccoons, so my wife felt it important that they were healthy, and eggs were added to the oatmeal cookie diet. We also kept a water pan nearby for them to drink and to dunk their cookies.

Raccoons will dunk anything in water if it is available. I did not expect that to be true for raw eggs, but it is. The egg clung to the paws, but slowly dripped down through the claws to the leg, then back into the pan. During the exercise the raccoon licked the egg off of their claws, paws, and legs. The surprise is that they manage to get every particle of the egg out of the water and pan. It is truly an entertaining and amazing exercise, albeit a mystifying one.

Nibs and Grundoone

There are two other raccoon events that stand out in memory. One has to do with my wife's interest in training Georgeena to ring a bell. At the time she was involved in social work with children and adults with learning disabilities. One of the fads making the professional rounds was operant conditioning, rewarding appropriate behavior. My wife taught Georgeena to alert us of her presence by ringing a cow bell that dangled at the end of a chain on our retaining wall. Whenever Georgeena rang the bell (by drawing up the chain and dropping the bell), she was given a cookie as a reward. Within a few days, Georgeena knew the drill well and got her generous reward each time she performed. Unfortunately, raccoons are nocturnal animals, so, the bell would ring at seven o'clock, ten o'clock, one o'clock, three o'clock, and so on till dawn. It occurred to both of us that the raccoon was now training us in sleep deprivation. The problem was how could we undo the raccoon's successful training? The answer is we did not. To this day, the progeny of the early visitors continue to return. Some of them are obviously related to Georgeena; they continue the drill learned by Georgeena and ring the bell to alert us that they are present. Unnerving as it is, our experience suggested

The first of many bell ringers

that operant conditioning works for both the short and long term. The second memory of recall relates to how brazen these critters can become, if encouraged.

+++

The Little Gentleman was precocious and gentle. He liked to be near the back door when the cookies were being distributed, but always waited his turn and took the cookie gently from our hands. The temptation to pet him was great but something no sensible person does. Gentle or not, he was a wild animal and could be dangerous. One evening while my wife was busy working on what was to become our garden, she left the back door open. Little Gentleman possibly waited longer than he found acceptable then marched into the house to find a cookie giver. Finding no one in the kitchen or living room he made his way to the bedroom. The system he was used to had broken down, and he was not about to tolerate being ignored. I was in bed reading when Nibs and Grundoone, my reading companions, came to a quick alert. There, standing in the bedroom, near the hall door, was Little Gentleman. He wasn't exploring or wandering, he was just sitting there watching me. He had located the only person available to take care of his sugar need. I got up, and the two of us walked out through the kitchen side by side and step by step to the area where the raccoons were normally fed. Little Gentleman stepped outside, sat down and waited to be served, which he was! Again, who had trained whom? But what difference did it make? My wife and I were beginning to establish a balance with nature that we both enjoyed even though it sometimes appeared to others that we were a bit batty.

The raccoons no longer dine on Mother's Oatmeal Cookies. They were weaned, reluctantly, from the cookies to day-old bread and then to generic dog food. This goes outside into two large metal bowls where, shortly thereafter, a festival of raccoons, fat and long tailed; skunks, and possum gather. Whatever is left over feeds the birds, the neighborhood dogs, squirrels, and whatever other fauna comes into our garden.

+++

Nibs and Grundoone shared their lives with many

43

other animals, but none more closely than Inky. He was not a handsome cat by any definition. His conformation was bad, his body far too big for his head and his tail too long for his great solid black body. Inky lived next door, more or less, for a vacant lot separated our house from his. Unfortunately, his own house was one with mental illness, anger, and other family problems that made his life unstable and uncomfortable. Inky gravitated toward comfort and being free of problems. Before he died he lived with four separate families in the neighborhood, one being ours, in his search for serenity.

We first came to know Inky when we discovered that he sneaked into our house early each morning while we were asleep and stole food left out for Nibs and Grundoone. Our bedroom windows pivoted out from the bottom. Inky would jump onto our front deck on the second floor of the house, make his way along an overhang, and come through the open window. We discovered his intrusion one night when he misjudged the opening and hit his head on the bottom of the window. The thud was loud, but his yowl deafening.

Inky, Nibs, and Grundoone lived together happily until we went to England on a Fulbright Scholarship for a year. Friends agreed to house sit for that year and take care of our animals as well. They were a young couple who were about to have their first child. Inky did not reckon on this. He lasted only a month after the baby arrived before moving on to more favorable circumstances with neighbors a few houses up the street. He remained with them until he died at a ripe old age, seventeen or eighteen we estimated. In his later years he was deaf, a little senile, and even more social than before. He would sit out in front of his current house and yowl to himself about nothing and everything. Inky was our first experience with a neighborhood pet, one that belonged to whoever he chose. His world was special and always accepting. Those of us who had the good fortune to know him also felt very special.

+++

The Nibs and Grundoone period of life on the hill covered many delightful and rewarding years. In her fifteenth year, Grundoone became seriously ill and died. Her loss was deeply felt by my wife, myself, and

Nibs. Within two months he died of kidney failure. My wife, the family romantic, insisted that he had lost his interest in going on without his life-long friend who always provided him with excitement and adventure.

Nibs and Grundoone taught us about many things, but none more important than the richness of experience that diversity promotes. Born into the same litter, the two could not have been more different in personality and animal behaviors, yet they complemented one another's lives. They proved daily the value and the importance of variety among all living things.

Grundoone and Nibs
"Diversity"

46

The Old Gumbie Cat

The Old Gumbie Cat arrived at our house in mid 1969. She really did not look like The Old Gumbie Cat described by T.S. Elliot. Her coat was not the tabby kind, with tiger stripes and leopard spots. Why we called her Gumbie is anybody's guess. But then, we are never sure why any of our animal friends end up with the names they do.

Gumbie was a mature tortoise shell with a coat generously sprinkled with black, orange and tan. Unlike many of our furry companions, she was not in the least neurotic. She was independent, loving, and an ideal household member from the time of her arrival. She showed up in the garden, marched to the French doors, thought things over briefly, and moved in. That was all there was to it. She had made up her mind to join the family, and did. She responded to affection with affection. As with most of the animals we have known, joining the carnival was their decision, not ours. Given the destiny that seemed to grace our household, we saw no reason to resist the decisions of the carnival crowd. Gumbie, as were all of the others, was welcomed to our house and its garden.

Not long after Gumbie's arrival, I received a Winston Churchill Fellowship from the English Speaking Union to study in Britain. We planned on a four-month leave and had to find someone to house sit for us. We hired one of our former neighbor's sons who was attending the University of California in Berkeley. Gumbie had a new companion for the next four months. It was during that time that Pippin, Punkin, and Peaches joined the family household.

Just before our scheduled return from London, our house sitter wrote us that Gumbie had produced a litter of four kittens in the bedroom closet. Mother and offspring were reported to be doing fine, and he had everything under control. When we arrived home, Gumbie took great pride in showing her litter to us, one pure white, one pure black, and two orange colored marmalades. Sadly, Snowy, the all-white kitten suffered from some form of severe nerve problem that made it impossible for him to stand or walk. He lacked the ability to balance himself. Efforts to help failed, and regretfully, we had to have him put to sleep. The remaining three kittens appeared healthy and rambunctious, an assessment that we later learned was seriously flawed.

+++

The kittens grew fat and strong, but after a few weeks we noticed that Punkin was beginning to have coordination problems. His front end worked fine, but the rear end just would not line up when he wanted it to do so. He was a kitten with two different systems for locomotion, one front, even and steady, and a rear one, disorganized, strong, but completely uncoordinated. Pippin, the black kitten, and Peaches, the other orange one, both appeared to be perfectly healthy.

Punkin's problems appeared serious. We took him to the veterinarian and were advised that if we could offer him a sheltered environment that he would prob-

49

The Gang of Three

ably prosper even with his coordination problems. With the exception of nerve damage, he appeared to be one healthy little cat. We talked it over and decided that if we were going to keep him he was going to lead as normal a life as we could offer him—no protected environment, only love, food, and care. He would have to learn to come and go as had all of our other animal friends. It was one of the best decisions we ever made.

Punkin may have had severe nerve damage in his rear end, but there was nothing wrong with his brain. He was one of several very intelligent animals who have lived with us. Punkin learned early that he was different, at least his world was, so he changed it to suit his needs. He learned among other things that speed and velocity enabled him to make his rear end go where the front end was pointed. So, when he wanted to go from point A to point B, he never walked; he thrust or burst forward at full speed. The adjustment worked well in open areas, but was a problem in more confined situations that tended to produce regular disasters—some big and some small. He would organize his body, charge it for full energy, and then at full momentum he would hurl himself toward his target,

50

Rushin' Punkin

generally an open door. Sometimes he made it through, but other times there was a large thud followed by an even larger meow, when he missed an opening and banged into a door frame. The meow, we always thought, sounded very much like a cat's version of "damn!" He generally missed one shot out of two, but there were occasions when the little guy retired at night with a bruised and sore head from a succession of failed charges.

Punkin was also a natural clown. He knew as well as we did that he could not judge jumps accurately, so when he jumped, he always did so with his front claws out as far as he could get them. He brought to mind an airplane landing on an aircraft carrier flight deck with all of his tail hooks deployed. We frequently found him hanging in a chair or drape that he had not cleared when jumping. He would wait patiently for rescue and then return to whatever journey he was on. We learned not to wear shorts around the house. Both my wife and I suffered the wounds of many Punkin crash landings before we learned to wear jeans when sitting around the house or garden.

51

Flying Punkin headed
for Juniper landing

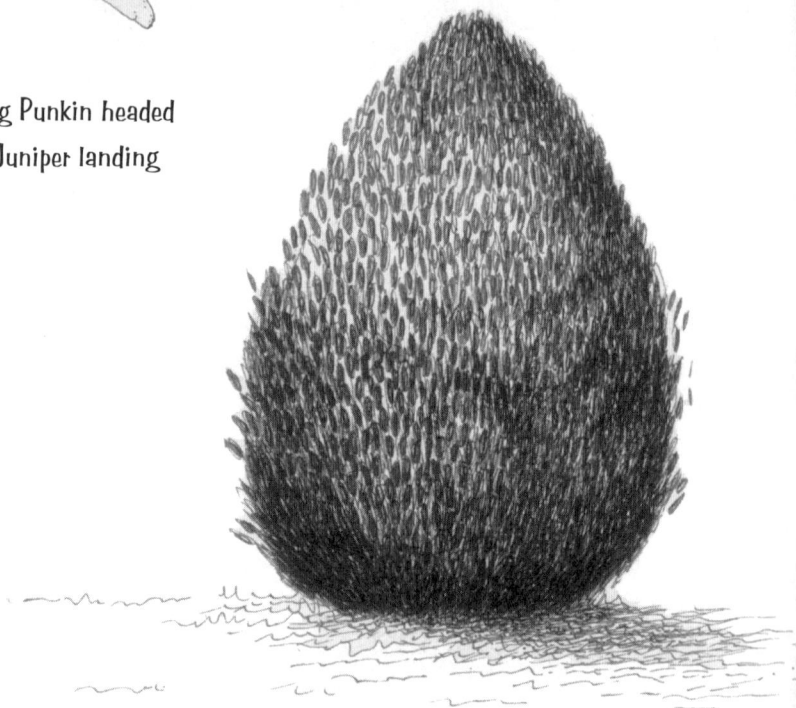

The Old Gumbie Cat

Punkin did not limit himself to overshots at ground level; he included second story jumps as well. Above our carport was a deck and three-foot wall. On too many occasions to count, our stout-hearted friend headed for the wall only to clear it and end up one flight down in the juniper bushes below. His Geronimo yell was a very loud EOOOW as he made his free-fall. His over shots on the bed were continuous. He loved to come up on the bed and in one of our laps when we were reading. He would charge the bed, sail through the air, over the bed and down the other side before braking his stop. Undaunted, he would turn around and spring back in the opposite direction, landing hooks out, reaching for something or someone to help him brake and land safely.

As the kittens grew, they played together and rough housed as if Punkin was just one of the gang of three. He never received special consideration from his litter mates, or his people friends. Being the house clown, he was always on center stage and seemed to know it. His world was special as was his ability to manage it. And, although his life was short, it was a full and enthusiastic life that constantly tested his abilities and determination.

53

+++

During the Gumbie era we had our carport enlarged. With the beginning of construction, several ramps were built so that workmen and materials could get up to the deck without going through the house. Punkin thought the ramps were for him. They were great play things intended for his amusement and adventure. The only problem was that the ramps were only twelve inches wide, adequate for man, but not a nerve-damaged kitten. Punkin needed two to three feet to safely negotiate the ramp for any extended distance. But to our surprise, and the workmens' delight, he mastered the ramps. They spent more time encouraging him than they did working on the deck. We knew that he had mastered something when we heard the shouts of the men followed by applause.

Peaches, joined his errant sibling in his adventures, but Pippin took life and limb more seriously and only watched his two litter-mates.

We thought about finding homes for the two healthy kittens, but not too seriously. Then one of my wife's work colleagues expressed interest in adopting a cat. She came to our house and fell in love with Peaches, who we believed to be a very large female. Later, his new owner informed us that this was not the case. When she took him to the vets to be neutered, she found out Peaches was a small tomcat. But, as in the Johnny Cash song, "A Boy named Sue," he retained his dignity, name, and always carried himself proudly.

+++

Bilbo arrived during the Gumbie era and lasted through the Oliver and Jenny period later. He came as a puppy with his mother, Laura, another neighborhood pet. His owner paid little attention to the two of them after her daughter moved away from home, so they were left to find love wherever they could. Bill spent his days wandering around the neighborhood visiting his various friends, which included virtually everyone within a block in any direction. Laura disappeared, and we really never knew her end, but Bilbo continued to share his time with anyone who would let him, which was virtually everyone. Warm and friendly, Bill did not score high on IQ, but he went off the scale when it

came to being sociable. As a result, everyone in the neighborhood was committed to looking after his interests, particularly with regard to his shoe fetish.

Bilbo stole shoes. He liked dress shoes, tennis shoes, men's shoes, women's shoes—all shoes. Everyone knew about his problem and had been victimized, so we all organized to deal with it in a creative manner. Collectively, we designated the local neighborhood mail box on the corner as the shoe retrieval center. Most days you could fine one or more shoes on top of the mail box waiting to be reclaimed by some owner. As one neighbor put it, "Bilbo was a retriever who specialized in shoes." He never chewed them, just stole them and left them around the neighborhood with his friends, almost as gifts. It was not a learned behavior; he seemed to have inherited it since he exhibited the characteristic during his puppy days when he was too small to even carry a shoe. As a puppy, Bill would show up at our back door dragging a shoe that was bigger than he was. Laura, his mother, would look at him proudly as he guarded the shoe, placing his head on it, and protecting it from disappearing. We were all convinced that he was born with the shoe fetish, a behav-

56

The Young Shoe Thief

Local Shoe Return Center

ior that followed him throughout his entire life.

Bill was an object to be cuddled by Punkin, Pippin, and Pepper. They loved to curl up in his fur, particularly on his belly. We were sure that they thought he was one of the litter by the way they accepted him in the house. Perhaps it was that he came as a puppy, and they were kittens at the same time. Bill never belonged to us, but the kittens didn't know it, and he certainly didn't. He would park himself in the house and stay there until bribed to go out, or on occasion, was physically lifted out by my wife and myself. Grown, he weighed about 100 pounds, all dead weight since he would go limp when we tried to remove him.

He was still a part-time member of the family when I was transferred to the East Coast. Before leaving Berkeley my wife had rented out the house with a stipulation that whoever rented our home also had temporary custody of the animals. Olli and Jenny were in residence and were to be treated as surrogate owners. For the most part we were lucky to find tenants who enjoyed our animal friends and did a very good job looking after them. They treated the house and animals with respect.

The Old Gumbie Cat

Our first renters were two young men who liked cats and were delighted to assume the responsibility for looking after them. Their unexpected shock arrived with Bilbo. We had failed to warn them about the neighborhood golden retriever. Shortly after my wife's arrival in Washington, D.C., she received a frantic call from the renter asking what was expected of them with regard to the large dog they found in the living room. My wife didn't understand their inquiry until they described Bilbo. As he frequently did, Bill had parked himself in the house and refused to leave. My wife explained to the callers that the dog was not ours, but everyone's. She suggested two remedies that we used: bribe him to go with a treat which we generally had available, or, just carry him out of the house. She assured them that he was friendly, and that was his problem. We later learned that he seduced them as he did everyone else, and became a temporary member of their household.

When we returned home four years later, Bill was still around, but he had been slowed by increasing age. His former owner had continued to ignore him, particularly as he began to suffer infirmities. But as he had done for most of his life, he simply moved in with friends across the street. They looked after him with care and kindness until he died. During his final year he continued stealing shoes, though half blind, deaf, and suffering from arthritis. Most of us miss the shoe return center on top of the mail box, and we all miss the world's greatest shoe retriever, who, in the end, must have gone out smiling at the amusement his shoe fetish generated for an entire neighborhood of friends.

+++

Gumbie, Punkin, and Pippin survived for almost two years before Punkin became seriously ill. Without much warning he began to suffer from respiratory and kidney failure that quickly resulted in his death. No one seemed able to explain his sudden physical collapse, but the vet had his suspicions. Shortly after Punkin's death we were visited by students from the veterinary school at U.C. Berkeley. They were a part of a research study looking into feline leukemia and had been referred because of the death of Snowy and Punkin. They suspected that all of the Gumbie line carried the disease.

We really did not need this news, let alone be reminded of the possible loss of Pippin and Gumbie. Within six months we lost them both to respiratory failure. As difficult as the experience was, we like to think that the information gained about Gumbie and her kittens contributed to the feline leukemia study and a subsequent vaccine to prevent such occurrences.

Peaches was another problem. Should we tell our friend about his possible inheritance and likely consequences, or just let nature take its course. We avoided a decision for some time, but finally decided that we had to tell them that Peaches was likely to suffer the same end as the rest of the gang. We learned that Peaches had already joined the litter and that her friend had been delaying telling us of his untimely death from a respiratory infection.

+++

Gumbie and her offspring were with us for only a few years, but as sorrowful as the experience became, it was one that we were grateful to have. Their time with us was informative, wonderfully funny, and until the end, very worthwhile. Punkin and his litter mates were an experience that neither of us would have chosen to miss, even knowing the end.

Gumbie and her kittens, sick and well, provided love, companionship, and happiness during their brief time with us. Punkin was special; he taught us how a handicapped kitten overcomes his limits and provides love and joy to those willing to encourage his unrestricted development. His life was neither barren nor dull, but, was in fact, vital, colorful and full of beauty. And Bilbo? His never-ending love and interest in shoes brought an entire neighborhood together as the friends the world's best shoe collector.

Number One and the Queen

It was over two years before we again added a four-footed friend to the household. No one had arrived on the scene voluntarily, and although my wife professed to be content with the passing wildlife, we were both beginning to miss the trials and joys of having an animal in the house. It was Saint Valentine's Day, which seemed like an appropriate day for me to get my wife a new friend. I thought she might like a Manx cat for a change, and located a local breeder in a nearby city. But, en route, for some reason I stopped by the local animal shelter, and without fully recognizing it, discovered our next family member.

+++

Oliver, or Number One as we later referred to him, was in one of the show cages at the shelter. He appeared to be about seven to eight months old, but no one knew for sure. His fur was extremely thick and soft even though he was short-haired. One of the attendants referred to his coat as chinchilla, an appropriate description. His performance in the cage was playful, bright, energetic, and affectionate. He looked good, but I had my mind focused on a Manx. I went on to the breeder's, but couldn't get the kitten out of my mind. The lady showed me her selection, explained the virtue and history of the Manx breed, and although tempted, none caught my fancy as the chinchilla back in the "local cat slammer." The more I thought of it, the more I became convinced that my wife deserved her own chinchilla cat. I returned to the animal shelter and bailed out the cat to become known as Oliver. We went home to surprise my wife, and she was delighted. I should quickly add that it was probably the last time he was affectionate or playful. Having made his escape, he reverted to his real self, a sly, reclusive animal who tolerated people only to the extent it was absolutely necessary. As it turned out, he was much older than he appeared. His limited development resulted in him being the world's smallest tom cat. Dripping wet and fully stuffed he never weighed over eight pounds in his

64

Oliver: The Valentine Boy

prime. Oliver gained his name from Oliver Twist, another orphan who was not what he appeared to be.

+++

Oliver's duration in the house on the hill was to include Jennifer, a.k.a. Jenny, Spot, Bear, Buffy, and later Boots. His initial time with us was problematic. He wanted to escape. Nothing was familiar, and he spent most of each day marking anything that did not already have his scent. It took almost two weeks for him to begin to settle in. He gained an additional nickname, "razor claws." We talked of him in terms of the joke about the swordsman who when he slashed his opponent appeared to have missed. Taunting the swordsman the victim said, "you missed me." The slasher responded with, "wait until you try to turn your head." On those rare occasions when Oliver took a swipe at us, we would cry out, "You missed!" His response was a blank stare while blood trickled from our hands, and then he would quietly walk away. Of all of the cats we have known, his claws were the sharpest, and his paws the fastest. Both of us carry the scars to prove it. He was not mean, but when he did not want to be bothered, he let us know in no uncertain terms. In spite of his unusual temperament he was a favorite who ruled, more or less, for the next seventeen years.

Olli was a hunter, specializing in garden snakes. He loved catching them as Grundoone had many years before, but he rarely killed them. He enjoyed sharing his squirmy playthings with us. We found them on the front porch, in the living room, and once when he was being his most creative self, in the bedroom. Effective as he was as a hunter, we never seemed to run out of a supply of grass snakes. They wriggled in our house throughout his life.

Oliver left no doubts about who was Number One on the hill. He established his position with people, cats, and dogs almost immediately upon meeting them. He was particularly assertive about who could join the family or family activities. He was downright brazen in demonstrating who was in charge. When a friend brought her large dog over for a visit, Olli would stalk the animal until he became bored with the game. Many a cat or dog was brought to cowering fright by the world's smallest tom cat. He also had what we came to

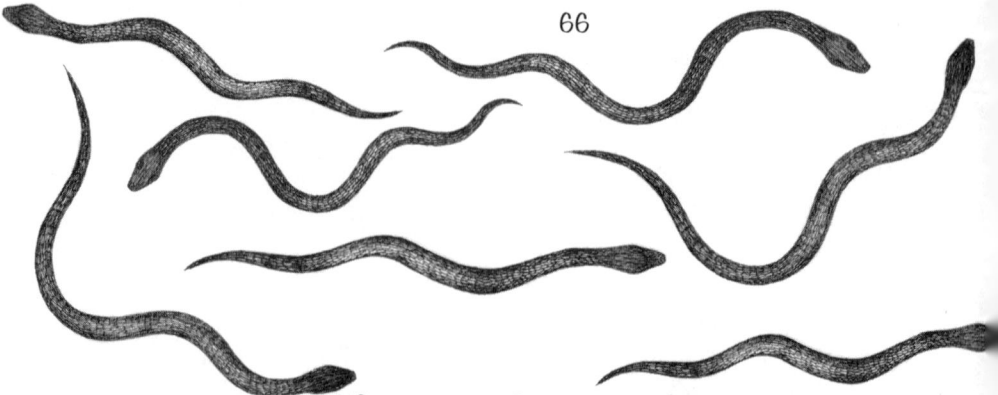

Grass snakes, A life-time supply

call the "sniff of indifference," a behavior reserved for large dogs or people for whom he had no time.

Shortly after his arrival we took him to the veterinarian to have him neutered. It was then that we learned that we had adopted a full grown cat who would never get much larger than he was. Olli's bane of existence was his fur coat. Always a center of attention because it was thick, soft, and beautiful, everyone wanted to pet and hold him—something he abhorred. Petting was sometimes possible, but to try and hold him was foolhardy and dangerous to hand and limb.

+++

Oliver had the run of the house for a year and a half before his lonely reign ended with the arrival of Jennifer. Our neighbors to the north of us asked us if we could take one of the kittens their cat had delivered. The ancestry included some siamese along with something much larger. We chose a gray tabby who was later to become Jennifer or Jenny after "Jennyanydots" from T.S. Elliot. She also became the "Queen" of the hill, a special name acquired when a friend commented

67

Jennyanydots, the "Queen"

on her regal walk. It was different from that of other cats. The term "pussy footing" was close, but really did not capture her special strut. She seemed to raise herself up on her toes and, touching the floor only when necessary, lift her great gangly frame, and glide across any surface with a regal elegance that was a marvel to behold.

We had always had our cats in pairs, something we think advisable. Inviting Jenny to live with us helped our neighbors, and it gave Oliver something to think about other than himself. Not having consulted with him, he was not in favor of the plan and let us know it the moment we brought her home. He would stalk Jenny, cuff her a few times and then ignore her. On the other hand, Jenny wanted a friend, and whether he knew it or not, it was going to be Oliver. She would charge him as kittens do, and even with rebuffs, kept trying to convince him that it was play time. She never gave up, and had several thrashings to show for it. For her, the most difficult times were those when he refused to acknowledge her presence and simply ignored her.

68

Punchin' out
the New Arrival

Number One and the Queen

Jennifer arrived home during her sixth week of life. She was still a small curly ball of fur that wanted to curl up with another cat, Oliver wanted no such contact. He would hiss, growl, cuff her, and she would come back for more. Determined and fearless, she confounded poor Oliver. She knew a cat when she saw one, and Oliver, mean or not, was the only cat around. The running battle went on for the first few months of her life, but she never gave up. In the interim, she grew and showed her unknown ancestry. By the end of the year, she was bigger than Olli and still growing. We always wondered if Olli had known how big she was going to become, would his attitude toward her have been different.

In her early weeks with us, we became her surrogate litter mates. She would jump onto the bed and slip under the covers, then make her way down to our feet. Why she did not suffocate, we never did figure out, but she would stay at the foot of the bed for hours if we gave her the opportunity. In our absence, she still made her way under the covers and down to the foot of the bed where, when we returned home, we would find a large breathing lump. This early imprinting

Jenny Grew Fast and Big

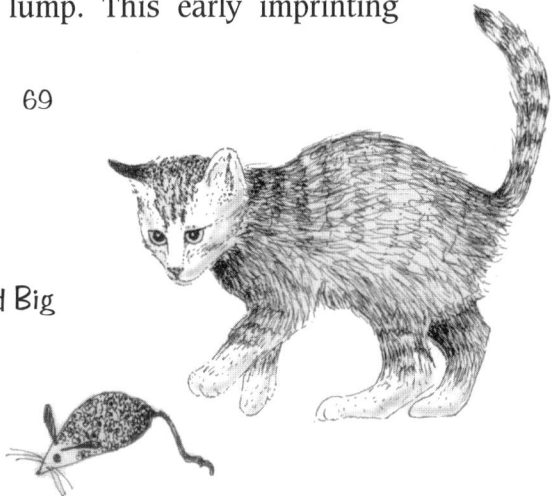

made her a regular on the bed at night. And, when she became too bored with the darkness and quiet, and being ignored, she would march up to the head of the bed and carefully select one of us to tap on the face. Her claws were never out, but her soft cold pads, gently struck our faces in a way that could not fail to get our attention. A few strokes of affection and she would return back to her place on or under the covers and curl up for the rest of the night. Clearly, we were her litter mates and were subject to all of the responsibilities that entailed.

+++

It is interesting what one can learn from their animals if they take the time to watch them. About one year after Jenny's arrival on the scene we awakened to snow. It had not happened before, and not since. We were familiar with hail, frost, and occasional sleet, but not snow. It was falling gently, covering our deck, and, because of the low temperature, remaining on the ground. By the time we were up and dressed, there was over an inch of unmarked snow on our deck. Both cats were interested, but Jenny was really excited. Opening the door, she charged out into this exciting new mystery to skid, slide, catch snow flakes, and in general act like a child playing. She was a genuine snow cat. Oliver took one step on to this soft, cold, wet stuff and wanted no part of it. It wasn't familiar, couldn't be trusted, and must be dangerous, he seemed to think. It was something to be feared and avoided. He turned around and retreated into the familiar and warm house. Not Jenny. She continued to run and prance in the snow, thoroughly enjoying the activity. For her it was something new, something to make friends with if possible. She wasn't about to miss the opportunity to explore this new experience to the fullest, and she did. When she finally retreated to the house she was thoroughly wet and cold, but could not have cared less. The one sad moment came later in the morning when the snow began to melt, and the special treat was disappearing. Jenny curled up by the door and watched the lovely snow turn to water, and then drain away to some new place that she could not go.

Our experience with our two friends taught us a great deal about them and also ourselves. Didn't we often behave as Olli? Weren't we often afraid of what was new, different, or the unfamiliar? We both agreed that from that day forward we would try and approach life as Jenny did, openly and with excitement about what was new. We were not always able to keep our promise, but over the years we have tried, and generally with great reward for our efforts. It was the first of many times that our snow cat taught us something about living life fully, with joy and excitement of the new and different.

+++

Jenny was intelligent, but also very stubborn. She had suffered a puncture wound under her chin from what we suspected might have been a gopher bite. She would not let us capture her and remained out until late that night. She finally came in with a great swollen abscess. We took her into the animal emergency hospital for the abscess to be lanced and a plastic tube inserted to drain the wound. When we returned to pick her up, she was wearing a surgical bonnet—a huge plastic cone collar that kept her from scratching the injury. When she walked she looked like a feline

72

The Queen's Surgical Bonnet

dinosaur, unsteadily walking along swinging her great bonnet from side to side.

Once home, we faced the problem of how to keep her inside without restricting Oliver's freedom to come and go. The bathtub appeared to be a perfect solution. It had clear glass sliding doors, allowing light in and permitting her to look out. We carefully arranged some pillows at one end of the tub for her comfort and put food, water, and a litter pan at the other end. We felt pleased with our creative solution for our ailing cat and her needed confinement. We did not take into account Jenny's creativity or determination, however. She wanted out. She was an outdoor cat and was determined to maintain her rights and freedom to come and go as she pleased.

It took her the better part of one day to figure out how to open the sliding glass doors on the bathtub. We were outside working in the garden when we saw her emerge from the house and head for the fence to the adjoining house to escape. My wife ran one way and I the other in an effort to recapture her. She was finally trapped, not by us but by the bonnet which prevented her from slipping through the narrow space under the fence. Reluctantly, Jenny returned to her private suite in the bathroom. This time the doors were wedged shut to prevent another escape. Our strategy worked until the next morning when the hooded monster once again succeeded in opening the doors and escaping. This time she came into the bedroom, jumped onto the bed and poked me in the face to let me know enough was enough. That day she went back down the hill to have the tube and bonnet removed. Once again she was free to join Number One and us when she felt like it.

Although Olli always remained Number One, even a grown Jenny occasionally got fed up with his bossy nonsense and would give him a good thrashing. Thereafter, peace would reign for long periods of time. Over the years, they became close and would hunt, sleep, and eat together. Olli learned to tolerate it. In the end, we think he liked the companionship as much as or more than Jenny, particularly in later years when we began to travel extensively.

Number One and the Queen

+++

My work eventually took me to Washington, D.C. for four years. We retained our home in Berkeley and rented it with several restrictions, the foremost being anyone renting the house had to accept our animals. There were three sets of renters of the house on the hill while we were away. The first were graduate students who looked after the house and the animals as if both were their own. Unfortunately, their plans changed the second year of the rental and they had to move. They were replaced by a family with a newborn child who proved to be a disaster, the family, not the child. The property manager ignored our rental contract in several ways when screening the new tenants. The most important breach to us, however, was failing to mention the clause about looking after the animals. These tenants appeared to dislike animals. Within a few months they had trashed the house and abused Olli and Jenny.

Olli, always self sufficient, survived this brief period reasonably well by spending much of his time next door with our good neighbors. Jenny, who was so dependent on her relationship with people, showed the damaging effects of the harsh rebuffs she received from the people who lived in her house. No longer trusting and affectionate, she began to avoid human contact whenever possible. Our neighbor finally alerted us to the situation, saying that she had expressed her concerns to the property manager to no avail. We contacted the manager and were told, for the first time, that there were some problems but that "things were improving."

My wife returned to California immediately to see for herself. She confirmed that there were many serious problems that would require her personal attention, the first of which was to terminate the lease and fire the property managers.

My job in Washington was extended for several more months, and we had an empty house and two cats in California. We began making plans for my wife to remain in Berkeley until the end of my contract when a friend of ours told us of a visiting professor from Germany in need of a place to stay and who might be interested in our house. He and his companion became our third and last tenants, and an ideal solution to our problem.

His companion was a psychologist by training and an animal lover by nature. She immediately recognized the need to rehabilitate Jenny. It began a process that took several months and considerable care on her part. Their first project was convincing poor Jenny that the "bad people" no longer lived in her house and that she was free to return. Their regime was simple and straightforward: tender loving care and reassurance. Even so, it was a long time before Jenny came to trust people again.

During the bad period, Jenny had learned to retreat to the roof of the house when things became too frightening. She used the skyway she and Olli played on in her youth. From the front deck there is a slanting wall up to the roof at about a forty-five degree angle. Both Olli and Jenny had raced up and down that wall in play as if it were a freeway to heaven. In his later years Olli learned to put out his razor claws and make his way back down the wall very carefully and always head first. Jenny, on the other hand, often had second thoughts about having gone to the roof when it came time to come down. She obviously did not like heights or the angle of decent. She would sit at the top, endlessly looking down and doing her calculations about how this was going to work. She eventually settled on what we came to call the "Jennipoo-slide." It was a sight to behold. First the cat would position herself at the edge of the roof and then slowly work her very large rear end, about sixty percent of her seventeen pounds, so that it was hanging out over one side. Then she would sink her claws into either side of the ramp and begin her slide. She had learned that gravity would do the work if she could just get her claws to serve as brakes on the downward journey.

Most of the time things went well, but there were others when her side-saddle approach got out of hand and she accelerated too fast. Whenever this happened, she would swing around to face the rapidly looming flowering cherry tree at the end of the slide. Trees were her safety net and her only reassurance for behavior that never changed, behavior that entertained us and

78

Jennipoo Slide

many friends who had the opportunity to see it. Today, her selected successor, Ms. Holly, uses the same style or approach to the wall while Oliver's successor, Boots, used the head first approach.

+++

It was not until after our return home from the East Coast that I learned Jenny liked classical music. When in the study or using the computer, I would turn on the radio, always tuned to the same local classical station. At first Jenny would only come in the room for short periods of time. She would groom, maybe walk over for a quick touch, and then move out. Her Queenly walk had disappeared and had been replaced by a furtive quickstep suggesting escape. But, following our last renter's regime, we continued to offer her reassurance and affection, on her terms. A few weeks after our return, she began to show an increased willingness to spend time with us. On one of these occasions she discovered the Barcelona chair, a leather chair that is comfortable for man and beast, located in the study. That chair was too much for her

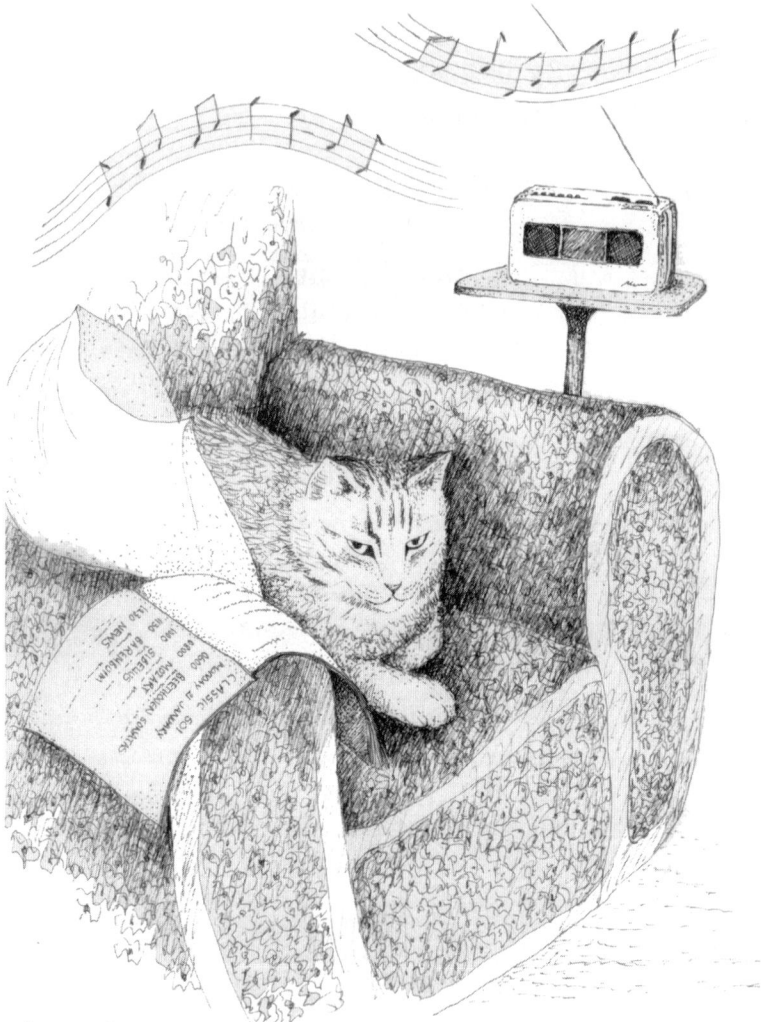

Classic Jenny

to resist, and she soon joined me every time I went in the room to work, but only when the radio was on. It was almost as if the music made the room safe and a place where she could completely relax. Before settling down, she would always offer me help by walking across the keypad for the computer. Having offered her constructive criticism of my work, and appearing to be completely satisfied with her contribution, she would curl up in what became "her chair" for the duration of that day's project. Olli never challenged her for the chair, and indeed, never offered me the same thoughtful company and assistance that Jenny did almost every day for the rest of her long life.

The differences between Olli and Jenny were great and yet, complementary. One was small and independent, and the other large and dependent on people. One could survive unkindness and neglect, even ignore it, and the other was terrorized by both. Seventeen years with Number One and the Queen helped us fully understand our obligation to them, and the consequences of our failure to honor all of those obligations. It also taught us that care and love overcomes the damage we do unknowingly. Second chances are rare; when they do happen, we like to take full advantage of the opportunity.

Binx and Spot

After our return home, from living in the east, we began walking daily in Tilden Regional Park, which is only a few blocks from our house. It was during these walks that we became acquainted with Binx, Buffy, and Spot. Binx was the first in order of acquaintance; he was a "loaner dog." A loaner is a dog that belongs to someone else, and is returned home to be fed and groomed by his owners, not unlike a grandchild for a grandparent.

Binx was a golden retriever. He lived two houses to the north of us in what had been a friend's house, but, now, was generally a student rental. This time, it was a family rental, an exception. The couple living there owned a matched pair of retrievers, one male and one female. They kept them in a large dog run in the front of the house. Both dogs frequently escaped from their pen and ran the neighborhood, having a glorious time with their short-lived freedom. Both were friendly and affectionate. While they were together, we had little to do with them except to provide short walks and return them home from time to time. One day we noticed the absence of the female. Binx, who had been a happy animal, became quiet and brooding. After the disappearance of his mate, he made little or no effort to get out of the dog run. He finally did, and it was then that we got to know him. We were not alone. During his short time on the hill the mailman, neighbors, garbage collectors, and even the cats and dogs came to know Binx, the friendly caged golden retriever who wagged his tail and greeted everyone with friendly barks.

We walked in the park every day and decided that we would enjoy the company of Binx if his owners had no objections. They were delighted at the prospect and assured us that anytime we wanted to borrow him, we could. We also learned that his mate had taken ill and died without much warning. Our daily routine changed to include picking up Binx before leaving for the park. En route, we met Buffy, a neighborhood dog who paid some attention to Binx, but only barked at us. He was

84

Binx

a nice little guy, about fifteen inches high at the shoulders, long blond hair, floppy ears, and at least partly owed his appearance to having cocker spaniel blood in him. We didn't know at that time how much a part of our life Buffy would occupy later on.

Our walks took us over three to five miles of isolated park trails each day. Along the way we would cross streams and pass a lake. Binx's blood lines clearly included being a water dog. We would be walking along a park trail after a rain and Binx would run ahead to a large mud puddle, flop in the water, and wait for us to catch up. The same was true of him when we crossed a small creek each morning. He would run ahead and we would find him belly down, paws out, soaking in the small amount of water running through the creek. The lake represented unrestrained joy. Anywhere along the lake edge where Binx could find easy access he charged in, often through several feet of mud. In other areas deep enough he would swim and fetch sticks. If we were willing to take the time, he would spend the entire morning fetching whatever you were willing to throw in the water, ball, stick, or even bottles. He loved it. The ducks were another matter. He

85

Binx, Water Dog

made only half-hearted attempts to chase them, but they rarely took him seriously. His delight with things wet meant that we spent a considerable time cleaning him up when we got home. He was frequently caked with mud from the lake. Once cleaned up he would hang around the house or garden until it was time to take him home to the dog run. As we came to know Binx, it seemed to take longer and longer to get him home, generally timed to be when his owners came back.

Binx was a lover. When he moved away, we greatly missed our friend. He had been a wonderful teacher. He again taught us about the importance of loving and trusting. He loved everyone who would give him the chance. His affection was offered unconditionally and without question. As a result, people responded to that trust with attention and love. He seemed to know the joy of living and sharing, something he did freely during his time with us at our house. Binx led us to Spot, the cat with the crooked face and tongue hanging out, who lived at the corner.

Binx and Spot

+++

Spot was one of a kind. We first noticed him when we were taking our daily walks up into the park with Binx, who knew where Spot hung out and introduced us one morning. He could always be found in the sunshine at a house on the corner. If the sun was out, Spot was curled up on the porch warming himself and appearing very happy with the world. We didn't know if he lived there, but his morning location was regular as clockwork. As soon as he saw Binx he got up, brushed himself off, and slowly walked out to the street to be petted and talked to about his fine coat and pleasant manner. Binx greeted him with a sniff and nudge with his nose; Spot responded by leaning into the dog's front paws and chest. With these preliminaries out of the way Spot would role over on our feet, gently bat at us to encourage more petting, and then scold us with a loud meow when we were about to take our leave. After we met him, he never failed to come out to greet us on our way to the park each sunny morning. And, as best we could tell, he never failed to greet anyone else who could be counted on stopping to pet and talk to him.

The Carnival of Animals

Spot could not be described as a show animal. There are many reasons for this statement and none cast aspersions on his ancestry. Sometime in the distant past he had been in a serious battle or accident that resulted in his lower jaw being broken. As a consequence, half of his teeth were missing, his jaw was lopsided, his tongue always hung out just a little, and he drooled. Generally white, he had gray marking across his head, a gray tail, and a great gray tabby spot on his left side in the midst of pure white. His fur was soft and silky, and his purr had the roar of thunder. He feared nothing. He was as quick to walk up to a strange dog and rub it as he was to approach a strange person. He was, by any standard imaginable, laid back; a cool cat in an earlier vernacular. He approached the world and everything in it as if it held nothing but good and kindness. For the most part, for him, he was right.

We knew Spotty casually for some years before we learned that he had been abandoned by his original owners after moving here from New Jersey. He lost his second adopted home when the lady at the corner house, where we had first met him, died. But Spot was a survivor, and as his situation changed he simply

Spot

moved on to his next home, which was next door. Our neighbor to the south had wanted a cat, but then Spot never asked permission to move in, he just did. As a result, he came to hang out with Oliver and Jenny, and later, Boots.

A year or so after Spot moved in with his new friends, our neighbor remarried. She was concerned about moving Spot to her new home out of the immediate area. Since he was already a part-time member of our carnival, we volunteered to take him into the fold officially. Already familiar with him, our two animals, Oliver and Jenny, accepted him as just one more member of the family. In part, this was the result of Spot's personality. Since everything and everybody loved him, or so he believed, he simply ignored any hostile overtures and pretended they never happened. And, after awhile, they never did.

One of my favorite memories of "Mr. Cool," A.K.A. Spot, occurred one week when my wife was visiting her parents in Long Beach. It was dinnertime. I had a calamari steak left over from earlier in the week and was going to make a sandwich. I didn't know then that

MENU
Calamari à la greque
Calamari steak
Calamari au poivre
HOUSE SPECIAL
Bob's Calamari
Sandwich

MOET &
CHAND

The Calamari Kit

calamari was one of Spot's all-time favorite foods. I was sitting at the table eating my sandwich and watching television. The calamari steak was larger than the bun that contained it and hung out over the side. I was enjoying my sandwich and watching the news when, without warning, Spot jumped on the table and took a bite out of the other side of my sandwich. I could not believe it. I put him down from the table only to have him return and quickly attack the calamari once more. So, I cut off some of the steak, from his side, and gave it to him. He finished it in a minute and wanted more. For a cat with no teeth, he managed to do a great job devouring the calamari. I cooked my last remaining steak. Spot immediately gummed it down, and still wanted more. From that day on, anytime we had calamari, Spot had his own steak, cut into small gumming sizes, of course.

Spot was a consummate survivor. He has suffered serious injuries, lost several homes, and had a thyroid condition which never slowed him down until his last year. He roamed his neighborhood domain with dignity and complete independence. We thought of him as Bustopher Jones, the cat about town..."the cat we all love and greet as he walks down the street."

He lived to be sixteen or seventeen, we think since no one really knew for sure. He was on his way to join us on the bed one night when, without warning, he quietly dropped dead, and moved on to another loving home.

We like to think that Spot found a warm sunny place where calamari is forever on the menu and that his happiness and love of life continue to let him "purr with joy and the roar of thunder" while many new friends pet and love him.

For us, Binx and Spot were special animals. From the beginning each sought and spent generous amounts of their time with the people who temporarily adopted them. Binx, unlike other dogs I have known, showed none of the distance that some estranged animals do. He would seek us out, put his head on our laps, and look us in the eyes for long extended periods of time. Spot was much the same way. Given the opportunity, he would find himself a lap, curl up, and loudly purr from the petting that he knew would follow. Both animals were completely trusting. They loved freely as if they had never had bad times. As with our other animal friends, love and companionship, were treasures that they knew must be shared to be enjoyed. Binx and Spot enjoyed life to the fullest while they enriched ours.

The Carnival of Animals

Dancing Friends and Pogo

The Carnival of Animals

Curly and Friends / Inky

The Carnival of Animals

Nibs and Grundoone

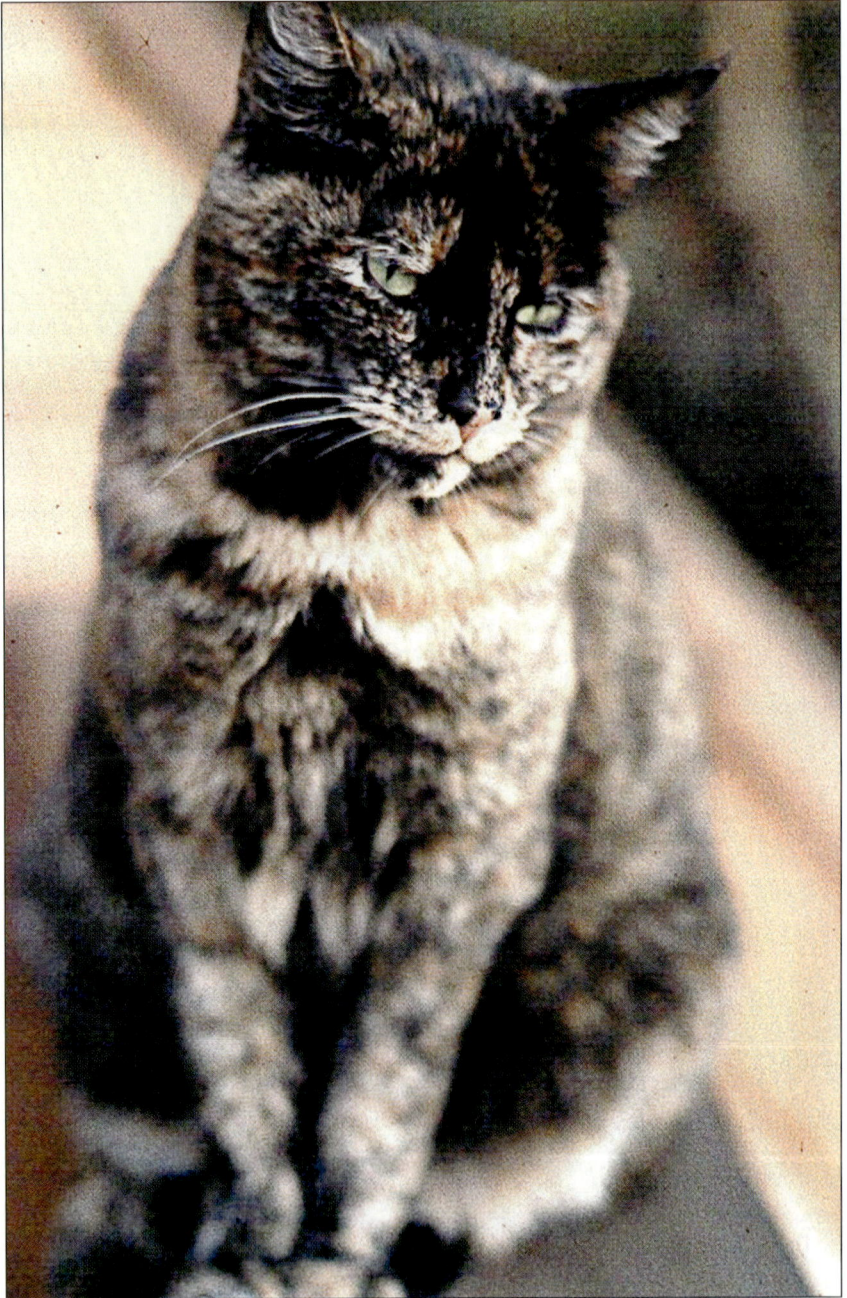

The Old Gumbie Cat

The Carnival of Animals

Peaches Pippin and Punkin

The Carnival of Animals

Laura and Bilbo

The Carnival of Animals

Olli and Jenny

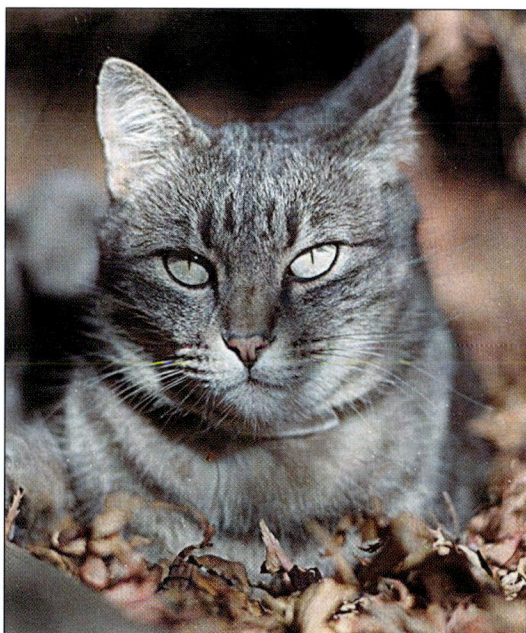

The Carnival of Animals

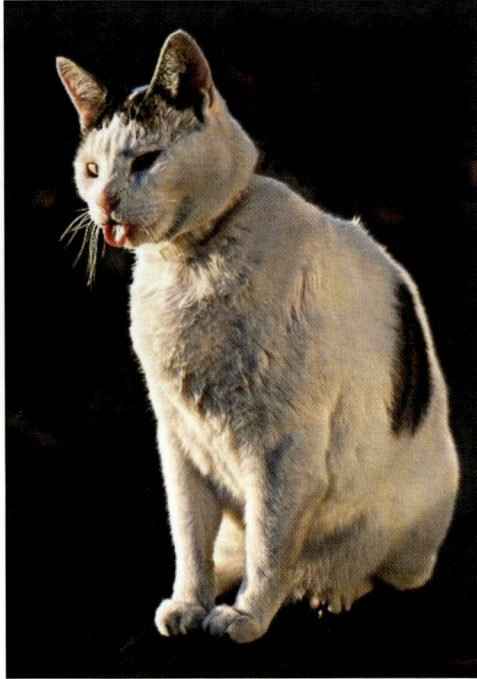

Spot and Binx

The Carnival of Animals

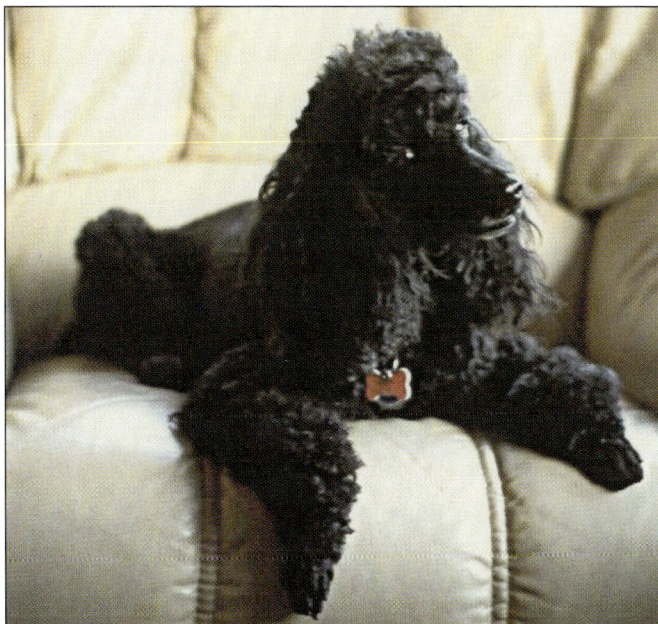

Beauty and the Bear

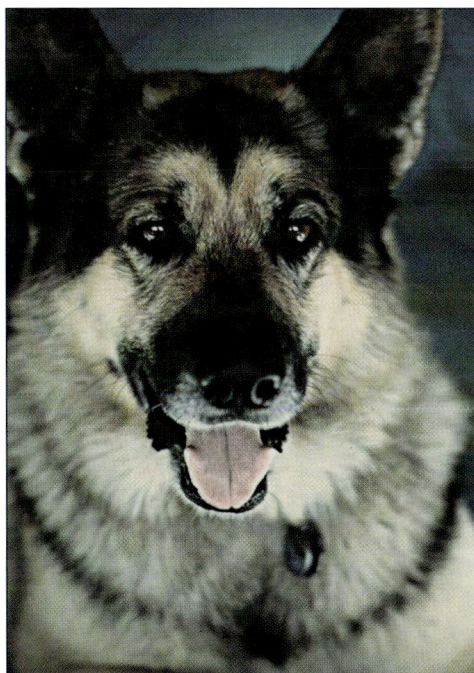

The Carnival of Animals

Holly and Boots

Toby, the Mayor, and Misto, the Magician

The Carnival of Animals

Buck, Doe and Fawn

Sammy: Holy Smoke! Have you seen the dogs with horns? From now on I am a housecat.

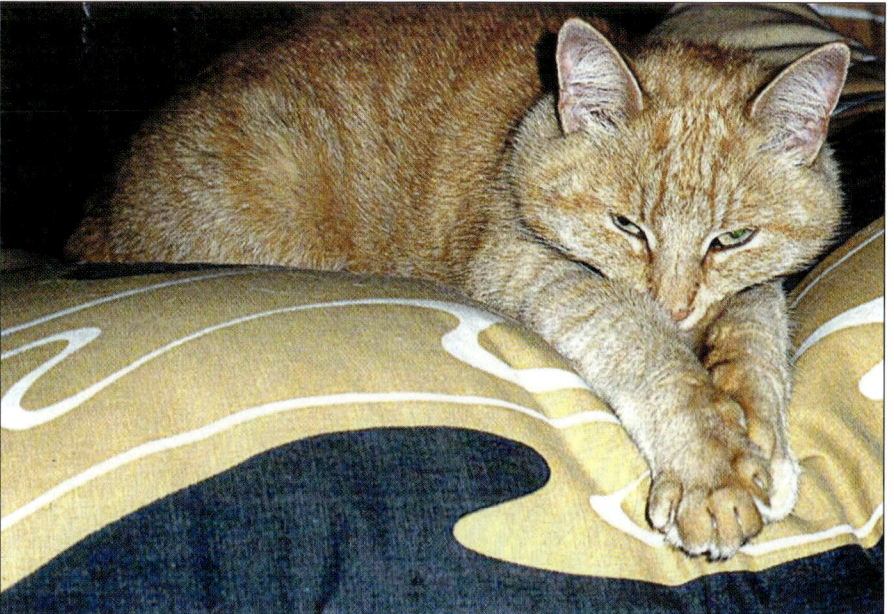

The Carnival of Animals

The Peanut Collectors

The Carnival of Animals

Tinkerbelle and Slippery

The Carnival of Animals

Buffy and the Bear

Buffy and the Bear

During August of the same year Spot moved in, we came home to discover a dog at our front door that looked miserable. He was big, but his bones stood out all over his body. He had a huge flea-infested bare spot on his rump that looked like blackened elephant skin. Very weak and placid, he nevertheless looked formidable. He refused to move, so everything, including us, had to go over or around him. The first few days of our acquaintanceship were carried out with great care and caution.

The stranger on our doorstep appeared to be mostly German shepherd, but with a malamute or husky mix. He obviously had been on his own for some time before settling in on our doorstep. He could barely move, and when offered food and water would take only the latter. We suspected that his arrival was not by

Flea infested stranger on our doorstep

accident. Every evening we put out generic dog food for the wildlife. He was not the first dog that had stumbled into this largess, and we suspect that he had been surviving on it for awhile without our knowing it. It was two days before he showed any interest in food. It was also about the same time that he showed me his one and only survival trick. When I approached him he would watch me very carefully and then raise his left paw as if to "shake hands." I do not know how successful the trick had been up until then, but from that time on it was a technique that reaped handsome rewards from whomever he extended a paw. Whenever he thought he was in trouble, the left paw would be extended in what always appeared to be a gesture of friendliness. It seemed that he knew one thing well: a good paw shake made anything right.

With his discovery, we did everything we could to locate his owner. We phoned the local shelters, posted his description around the neighborhood, and read the local newspapers for a missing dog. When we called the animal control people to report our find, they apparently thought we were reporting a stray. Shortly thereafter a young man with a frayed rope showed up to take the stranger away. But, our stray, who had been glued to the front porch for days, disappeared until after the threat of capture had gone. Whatever sense he was using, it worked well to alert him of any danger. My wife thought I had called animal control and was threatening to put me in the dog house for an extended period. She broke down in tears, sobbing that no one would adopt a dog in such bad physical condition. She argued that we should keep him, but only long enough to get him well and back into good condition so that someone would take him home with them. Eight years later at 106 pounds and with a fully healthy coat of hair, we were still trying to get him back into shape so that someone would adopt him. Thus began the era of Buffy and the Bear which overlapped Number One, Queenie, Spot, Boots, Holly, and Toby by several years.

+++

Not having had a dog living with us since childhood, we had much to learn and Bear was a very good experience to teach us how much we had forgotten. We learned among many things, that offering a dog a home is not unlike taking on the responsibility of a two or three-year-old child who never grows up. He needs attention, companionship, exercise, discipline, structure, feeding, doctoring, training, and all of the other things required when socializing a new member of the family.

In spite of his miserable physical shape, he was going to be a member of the household temporarily and needed to go to the vet for a physical examination. We didn't know if he could be trusted around other people, or would even ride in a car. Those were problems to be faced in the future. For now we needed to deal with the fleas that swarmed all over this poor animal. We desperately needed to get his infestation under control, for his sake and for ours. After the third day, and with great care, I got the visitor up into the back garden and began covering him from one end to the other with flea powder provided by our vet. The dog patiently suffered the indignities of home doctoring and looked like a gray ghost when we were through. I also hosed down the front porch and sprayed it with an approved flea and tick spray. And, of course, my wife knew that the door mat was too small and uncomfortable, so we provided him with a cotton rug that she found at a local discount store. We were doing all of this to get the animal in shape so that someone would adopt him.

The fleas came under control quickly, but there was a serious question about whether or not his coat would ever recover from the damage caused by his allergic reaction to the flea bites, causing the blackened elephant looking skin on his rump. We really needed to get him to our veterinarian so that he could assess his general condition.

+++

Soon after the dog arrived on our front porch a dog owner friend of many years stopped by to see and give us advice about our new boarder. One sight and she agreed that we needed to get him to a veterinarian for a checkup. To her, he looked in miserable physical condition. She too wondered if he would accept being restrained or would ride in a car. He answered the question a few days later. Our friend stopped by on her way to the park to run Beauty, her miniature poodle. She wanted to know if my wife wanted to go along. She agreed and got in the car. They headed off up the street with our doorstep foundling running along after the car. Our friend stopped and backed down to the house and the dog followed. My wife got out of the car to open the rear door on the passenger side while our friend rolled down the window on the driver's side to tell me that they were going to try and convince the stray to join them. Without a moment's hesitation he leaped through the window on the driver's side and on to the front seat next to her. Then he jumped into the back seat next to Beauty. There they sat, side by side seeming to say, "let's go." We no longer had any questions about whether or not the dog would ride in a car; we couldn't keep him out thereafter.

Both our friend and Beauty quickly were included in our foundling's new pack. His special relationship with our friend was always demonstrated by his greeting when she would arrive at our house. It was a special greeting reserved only for her. He would rush up to her, stand on his hind legs with front paws on her shoulders and give her the biggest lick one can imagine. She always braced herself against the nearest wall to avoid being knocked down by his charge. Our friend was the first person to rough-house with the dog on the floor. The two of them would butt heads, push one another, and make playful physical contact. The bonding that developed between the two lasted throughout the dog's time with us. On those occasions that he did not accompany us on an overnight or weekend journey, he would stay with our friend and her dog, Beauty. He always seemed to look forward to the visits as if he was going on holiday. Perhaps he was.

+++

Once we knew the dog would travel, he was off to our vet for his physical check up. We were advised that he had been on his own for a long time, was underweight, and had a severe allergic reaction to his flea infestation. The vet doubted that the bald spot on the rump would ever grow hair again, but that remained an open question. He encouraged us to continue the flea treatments, give him vitamins, and see that he had a good diet for a senior dog. The animal's age was estimated at about eight years based on his gray muzzle and general conformation. Unfortunately, his teeth were of no use to determine age because he had worn them down from chewing rocks. Happily, in time the

117

hair did come back, and the sixty pound weakling grew to 106 pounds of muscle and stamina. It also became apparent in a short time that the dog was born to be a sled dog. He insisted on pulling powerfully anytime he was on a lead. To the amusement of our neighbors we were dragged up and down every hill and road in Berkeley. We provoked smiles for anyone who observed us trying, unsuccessfully, to restrain a frustrated sled dog dragging us along behind him.

There were a number of incidents of note during the dog's early days with us. But the one I remember most is the night my wife decided that it was too cold for him to remain outside on the front porch. We brought him in and blocked off the dinning room for him. We used bar stools to prevent his gaining access to the rest of the house through the living room or kitchen. About three o'clock in the morning, we were awakened by strange banging sounds, noise that suggested burglars breaking in. I cautiously got up and moved slowly toward the sounds, not sure what I was going to find. I switched on the kitchen light and there stood the burglar, on all four legs and wearing a bar stool around his neck. He had decided to

The Bungling Burglar

Olli

Jenny

Spot

steal a snack from the cat dishes in the kitchen. In breaching the barricade he had stepped through two of the four legs of the stool. He had managed to get his large head and one of his legs through the opening, ending up wearing the stool as a complicated collar. His new collar was acting like a battering ram every time he moved in any direction. I interrupted my laughing long enough to extract him, which was not done easily. It was an amusing sight for us, but not the dog. He looked sheepish about the whole thing and obviously would have preferred to forget the matter. We took the barricades down, and from that night on the dog had the run of the house at night since he was house trained. The new addition to our family would stay in the house along with Olli, Jenny, and Spotty. Given the importance of that decision, we decided he needed to be trained and have a name other than "dog."

We located a local dog trainer who offered weekly sessions on weekends in a nearby town. We took dog in for his first session, and as it turned out, his last. The trainer was demonstrating how we could maintain some control through the use of a pinch collar, when to her surprise she was standing eye to eye with our new friend. She had pinched in on the collar to get him to respond to a command, and he turned, stood on his hind feet and put his front legs on her shoulders and growled. In any other circumstance I had never been able to get him to look me in the eye; he always dropped his head and looked away. But now, he wanted there to be no doubt about his message, "enough was enough." He would not suffer pain. As of that moment, our dog was no longer in training. The instructor suggested that he had been abused and that we should take care in whatever future training we undertook, which she speculated would take a long time. She was absolutely right in her prediction.

We bought a standard choke collar for the dog and began to take him out for thirty minute sessions in an isolated area of Tilden Regional Park. Heel, sit, stay, etc., interested him for about fifteen to twenty minutes, but then treats be damned, he had enough and would play dead dog by falling on the ground and going absolutely limp. His bribe was an offer to run free in the park for awhile or go home, both being equally acceptable to him. We never did complete his training, but he did agree to accept a limited number of commands from us.

We told our long time friends who live in San Andreas about our nameless addition to the family. They were surprised, and questioned our sanity at taking on this responsibility at our age, but they were eager to meet him and proposed that we bring him to their summer cabin at Silver Lake for a naming party. Silver Lake is about a four hour drive from Berkeley. It was during this trip we learned that dog loved to navigate. Our car was a small hatchback with a rear seat that folded down to form a large open trunk area. Although he was able to stand, his large, upright ears were pressed flat against the roof for most of the journey. He stood looking over my shoulder to check the road ahead, the scenery, and everything else along the way. By the time we arrived at the cabin, he could hardly keep his eyes open, but he was trying. That stance became his trademark whenever traveling with us. He would stand with his head over my shoulder, looking out through the windshield to keep us on track. In his mind he had a responsibility to be the world's finest navigator.

Buffy and the Bear

On arrival at the cabin we found our friends sun-bathing on the lakeside dock. They greeted us with the observation that this was a large dog, even handsome if you ignored his barren rump. They had expected a mangy, nondescript mutt, not an Alaskan sled dog. Since this was to be a naming party, we compiled a list of proper names, descriptive names and, finally, titles: King, Prince, Duke, Baron, etc. Baron had a nice lilt to it, we all agreed. And for once, dog showed a glimmer of interest, even though short-lived. Baron it was! By this time we were caught up in the naming exercise and took a further step. Baron should have a name that was titled, proper and descriptive. The German proper name for August, the month of his arrival, seemed appropriate. In keeping with his German ancestry, and our surname, Smith, he became the Baron August von Schmidt. To celebrate we opened a bottle of cham-pagne. In the excitement, Baron slipped and fell into the lake. The distance between the dock and the water level was more than he could handle, so we all lent a hand in pulling him out while chanting, "you are chris-tened Baron August von Schmidt." The Baron was not at all amused by this nonsense and demonstrated his disdain by showering us all with water as he shook it

123

"Baron August van Schmidt"

out of his thoroughly wet coat.

Pleased with the selection of a name we were bothered by the practicality of how one calls his dog late at night. Baron August von Schmidt did seem a mouthful, and even pompous. Soon his official name was shortened to Bar or Bare or, more naturally, Bear. And so, this is how the Baron came to live with us, and how he became the Baron known as the Bear.

+++

Bear had been with us for a short time when we began to take him for walks in Tilden Regional Park. Our normal route took us by Buffy's house in the next block. Our first encounter with this little dog was in his role as protector of his household. When we walked past his house with Binx, our loaner dog, he would bark ferociously and check us out through a hole in the hedge. Before we knew his real name, we referred to him as Blondy because of his long, golden hair. He did not become an honorary member of the family until Bear arrived on the scene.

Buffy's family was away from home during the day,

124

Buffy checking us out
through the hedge

and he was generally in his front yard protecting it and checking out every passerby. Although his first encounter with the Bear was not much to mention, the usual sniffing and checking each other out, Buffy had not barked or gone into his protective mode. Bear quickly became bored with the introduction and resumed pulling my wife on up the street. But from that day on, Buffy would come running out to greet the Bear, and incidentally us, with his bushy tail twirling in the air like a gyro scope. He never wagged his tail, only circled it rapidly above his rear end in a whirling motion.

A few days after the two dogs met, Buffy decided to join us on our walk, something that he had never done before. He would prance alongside us as if he were a member of the pack which he knew he was and we were soon to learn. Everyone we passed commented on what a fine little friend the Bear had. Buffy loved the attention, and with a twirl of the tail made sure he got even more. Together they would run along the fire trails acting like puppies, sniffing everything with intense interest, sometimes routing out quail and squirrels, and on at least one occasion chasing a deer, for which they were admonished.

Upon returning to our street at the end of the walk, Buffy would turn to the left to go to his house and we to the right to go to ours. Before long, however, it must have occurred to Buffy that no one would be at his house until about six o'clock that evening; so, he began spending his days with the Bear, and incidentally, us. Thereafter, he would turn to the right and lead the parade to our house and join the carnival of animals.

Because Bear always seemed to find mud on our walks, his undercoat, more often than not, was thickly coated with the stuff. So, we developed a routine, particularly after walks on inclement days. He hated it since it involved water and a hose. We hosed down his underbelly, legs, and feet to get off mud. Bear did not approve of this routine at all. Not only did he dislike getting wet, he was fearful of the hose. He eventually learned to tolerate the indignity once he realized that it would be followed by a toweling down and brushing. During the interim he did take his revenge when, thoroughly wet, he would shake himself vigorously splattering us with water. Then he was ready to jump on the patio table, wag his tail, and notify us that it was OK to get on with the rubdown. It did not take Buffy long to figure out how to avoid the hose while still showing up for the grooming session. He frequently outmaneuvered the Bear to be first on the table and first for grooming. My wife always took the time to comb out his long matted hair and assure him that he was a fine handsome dog and a great friend of Bear. Buffy was in his glory when being groomed.

Their longtime relationship was quite remarkable. Buffy, who probably weighed only thirty-five to forty pounds, took it upon himself to be Bear's bodyguard. Whenever a strange dog approached, Buffy, who was never on a lead, (Bear was), would intervene, literally placing himself between the Bear and the other dog in order to prevent his approaching. In the rare fights that did occur, Buffy was always the first into the fray to protect his friend. The behavior was regular and obvious. It was also deliberate and not just a chance occurrence. With Beauty, our friend's Poodle, his behavior was even more bizarre. Buffy would not stay in the house with Beauty and the Bear. If Beauty came to visit, Buffy took off in what can only be described as a huff. Jealousy was a significant part of the behavior. Under normal circumstances, Buffy always acted like he lived with us, which he did, on a part-time basis.

Buffy's schedule with us was from 9 A.M. to 5:30 P.M., Monday through Friday. Weekends he spent with his people. When his nightly departure time came, Buffy would get up from wherever he was napping, come by each of us to let us know it was his time to go, and then slowly walk down to the street, turn left and head home. About fifty yards up the street he would stop and turn around to see if we were watching, and if we were, he would bark once, start his gyro-driven tale in a great circular motion, and continue up the street at a fast trot. His internal clock was unfailing. He knew when to go home and on weekends and holidays, to stay home—except for the walk. That he made with us seven days a week, but with the difference that he returned home when we had finished. Weekdays, if we slept in, he was here at nine o'clock in the morning to bark and let us know that it was time to go for our walk.

Buddies at rest

Buffy and the Bear

Although Bear's friend chased every other cat he met, he never bothered ours. Buffy seemed to enjoy the chase, but seemed uncertain what to do if he was ever successful in catching something. He was a friend of our family for a number of years before age began to show its effect on him. On our later walks to the park it became obvious that Buffy could no longer handle the hills and would slow down to a crawl or even on occasion, turn back. When it first began to happen, my wife or I would pick him up and carry him up the hill so he could continue with the Bear. But later, when even this was too much for him, we avoided going by his house so as not to tempt him. Nevertheless, each day, he would come down about the time he knew we would come home and want his grooming before curling up for the remainder of the day. I would drive him home at his usual time and leave him in his front yard to greet his people when they came home from work.

The day before our little friend died, I found him in the street, headed down to see us. He made it as far as he could, but he had fallen and was no longer able to stand. I carried him to our house to spend the day and drove him home at his usual time that night before leaving him curled up on his front porch. The next morning Bear found him exactly where we had left him, stretched out peacefully and looking as relaxed as he had always been with us. Surprisingly, Bear showed no interest in the the body in which Buffy's spirit had lived with such vitality. It was as if he recognized sooner than I, that the Buffy we knew was gone. The shell before Bear was not the Buffy who had befriended him and protected him on so many occasions. From that day on, only his spirit would accompany us on our walks through the park. Bear's acceptance of the realities of death seemed more developed than mine that morning. My wife and I had become very fond of the Bear's protector and friend. We missed his enthusiastic morning greeting, the whirl of the gyroscopic tail, and the excitement with which he greeted every day, and we still do.

+++

During the first year Bear lived with us we were simply the people who treated and fed him. We also restrained him and interfered with his freedom to go back on the road. He was gentle and cooperative, but he showed no evidence of our imprinting on him. He was obviously not yet a member of our pack, even though Buffy was. That did not happen until a year later when we were visiting my wife's parents in Long Beach. The Baron was always quiet and unprotective of either of us, even when strangers came close. It was that Christmas in Long Beach that he assumed the role of our protector. He was being his usual disinterested self in the parking lot of a local grocery store when some shoppers came close to the car. He went berserk. The car shook with his barks and charges at the poor strangers who were frightened out of their wits. Whenever he began barking he always jumped with his front feet several inches off the ground. His weight brought him down with a loud thud and shaking of the car. We too were startled. Our docile quiet moose of a dog had become a ferocious, threatening beast. He literally rocked our car and frightened everyone within a radius of fifty feet. From that day on his relationship to us changed. The house and all who inhabited it were his personal responsibility and had to be protected from harm. For him, protection meant no more than ferocious barking and jumping. He almost never attempted to bite or snap at anyone.

131

Once Bear decided we were members of his pack or him ours, he initiated another behavior that was part instinct and part fun. Bear rarely played. Our friend had tried get him to chase balls with Beauty, but without success. His only game with her was head butting on the floor of our living room. We all thought that, for whatever reason, he had simply never learned to play as a puppy. We were surprised therefore when we returned home that Christmas and Bear introduced us to his game we called "snakes." It always began when we pulled back the covers on our bed in his presence. Before he had bonded with us that Christmas he would join us in the bedroom each night and curl up on the floor. After Christmas, his behavior changed. He would come into the bedroom and watch us straighten the bed each evening. He had limited his interest to just watching for the most part. Then one night, he decided we needed help since we obviously were not clearing the pack den of snakes. He jumped on the bed and began pawing the covers in all directions. The harder we tried to restrain him, the harder he pawed until he had the covers all collected in the middle of the bed—first one direction and then another until he had accomplished his instinctive task. We tried hard to hold the covers in place, but the harder we tried, the more enthusiastic Bear's pawing became. We assumed that it was associated with his wolf ancestry and the need to secure the den, but, then again, perhaps it was only a game he invented and enjoyed playing with us. It never ended until all of the covers were piled in the center of the bed. Only then would he jump down and let us pull the covers up on the bed. He did this with us every night until it was no longer possible for him to do so. Near the end he could no longer jump on the bed so we helped him up. Never forsaking his responsibility to protect the den and the pack, he struggled until he felt he had done his duty and cleared our bed of his imagined danger.

His favorite position for protecting the house was the front deck from which he could look down on everyone and everything. Particular targets for attack were refuge collectors, mail persons, meter readers, and especially, United Parcel Service people. Actually, it was not the people so much as it was the vehicles they drove. The noise was the trigger, be it the squeak of the mail person's car or the roar of the UPS truck. They all became used to this hulking threat and saved candy

133

"Formidable Bear"

and tennis balls to throw up to him. They even sent him holiday greetings. We never had the heart to tell them that he did not know how to play ball, something that seemed to amaze him when Beauty or Buffy played in his presence. On the ground, Bear was a formidable looking animal, but from fifteen feet up, and with only his big head and shoulders showing, he was even more impressive and, for the uninformed, frightening to behold. Few, except maybe Buffy, knew that at heart he was a lover and not a fighter.

+++

Given the option of flight or fight, Bear would always run away. The one exception to this pattern was with our longtime neighbor to the north and his miniature schnauzer, Max. Early in Bear's stay with us, I had made the mistake of inviting him to walk with me to their home to return something borrowed. The house has a fence around the entrance that is about four feet high. I left Bear outside the gate while I went to the front door. Max came out of the house yapping and barking with his usual greeting to all visitors. Bear obviously read this behavior as threatening, but did not follow his usual practice of fleeing. Bear jumped the fence and attacked Max. He had him in his mouth shaking him like a rag doll. Although it was only a few seconds before I could stop him, it seemed much longer. Much to all of our surprise, Max weathered the attack with only minimal damage, but his owner was marked as a permanent part of this encounter. Thereafter, whenever Bear heard our neighbor and his dog pass by on their walk he would charge to the front deck and begin his attack stance of jumping up and down and barking. One day, unbeknownst to me, the back door was open when they came by. Unfortunately, the Bear knew. He started his barking on the deck and then charged the back door. Before I could stop him, he was down the steps, through the carport, and up the street after his adversaries. The owner interceded to protect Max. For his efforts, Bear pinched him on the side, leaving a substantial red welt. Our toothless friend could not really bite with those worn teeth, but he sure could pinch. From that day forward the man and his dog were marked as one in Bear's mind. The man's wife could pet the Bear, just as everyone else in the neighborhood came to do, but not her husband. He was the enemy.

135

"Max"

Wisdom being the result of experience, he would not get near the Bear. So, for the next seven years, whenever Bear and I passed them on their walk, we tried to keep as much distance between the Bear and Max as was possible. I even walked Bear out of sight of Max to avoid any confrontation. But, hard as I tried, my attempts were generally futile, for whether or not Bear could see them, he knew when his nemesis was near. Max remained Bear's sworn enemy to the last. In this sense, our neighbor and his dog were very special to Bear; they were the only ones Bear ever met that he did not like. I never did convince our neighbor that it was Max and not him that Bear disliked.

+++

In our early walks together through Tilden Regional Park, the Bear and I would go for miles on the fire trails and hiking paths without meeting anyone. I got careless about keeping Bear on a leash. For the most part our long walks were without incident, but from time to time we would encounter other dogs off leash, who Bear, more often than not, would ignore if they would let him. But pushed, he would fight, and there were times when I found myself in between flying teeth, feet and fur, trying to stop the altercation. In these instances, both the aggressor and the aggrieved seemed happy for the intervention and rarely turned their hostility to me, and I returned home muddied, but not bloodied by the struggle. For the most part, Bear showed good sense when confronted with possible adversaries by ignoring them, whenever possible. Having him on a leash helped us both do that.

A classic example of this was the day that Bear and I met another Max on the trail. This Max was a huge mastiff who was running free along the route we were heading. Bear took one look and decided this was a confrontation that he preferred to avoid. Without warning he took off up-hill even though he was on his leash. I was dragged along behind whether I wanted to be or not. Having been dragged through wild berry bushes and poison oak I was in no mood for this encounter either. Poor Max was hot on our trail when I finally stopped the Bear, turned and shouted "STAY!" as loud as I could. Fortunately Max was intimidated by people or trained well enough to get the message. Poor Buffy was trying to intervene, but the whole thing had happened too fast for him. Following my shout, Max had stopped and Buffy caught up and put himself between the huge dog and us. As unbelievable as it seemed, Buffy backed off the mastiff. About the same time, the dog's owner, a twelve-year-old girl, arrived on the scene. She was running after Max trying to call her dog off. She took the whole scene in stride and without missing a beat told me with great pride about her great "humongous" dog Max. It occurred to me then; maybe it was not schnauzers that Bear disliked, but only dogs named Max.

+++

Bear was a working or herding dog, but he was not a water dog. He hated water in any form be it from the hose, lake, or ocean. We first learned this on my wife's birthday. It was a beautiful day, and we decided it would be nice to go over to Marin and enjoy the beach. We got there only to discover that Bear had reservations about sand, but was dead set against the surf that attacked him and got him wet. He wanted nothing to do with it and made every effort to leave. He acted miserable and frightened the entire time we were there. He snapped out of it only when we took him up on the

"I hate water."

Marin Headlands where the water could not get at him. High above the surf, things seemed a bit more safe. His pleasure only increased when it was time to leave and he beat us back to the car.

We further confirmed his aversion to water when we took him by the local lake in Tilden Regional Park on one of our long walks. We enjoyed walking around the lake, and Buffy enjoyed swimming in the lake. The Bear liked neither. Water was water in any shape and even though this water didn't attack him like the ocean had, it was water nevertheless. Bear patiently watched his small friend Buffy enjoying himself swimming, but he would not venture one step toward him or the water. It took us almost five years to convince him that bathing was good, particularly since it was always followed by grooming. Some instincts die slowly, and his resistance to water waned at a glacial pace.

+++

Bear's survival, was to a great extent, due to his good luck in finding the generic dog food we put out for the raccoons and other wildlife in our garden.

Because of his poor health when adopted by us, his diet changed to an upgraded dry food and a good canned food. He thrived on this for a couple of years before my wife became concerned that his diet was inadequate. "After all," she said, "our friend cooks up chicken for Beauty." She proposed her idea to our veterinarian who agreed that chicken was a good diet for a dog. Her clincher in the argument was that frozen chicken parts were actually cheaper than canned dog food, an argument that was only true if you discounted the weight of the bones. In any event, the Bear was soon dining on shredded baked chicken and dry dog food. He approved of the change and never once objected.

Each week we would scour the paper for the lowest price on frozen chicken parts, which were generally about thirty-nine cents per pound. Canned dog food ran well over sixty cents per pound. Once we had located the lowest price it was my job to get two or three bags for preparation. My wife, generally on Sunday, baked the chicken, shredding it, and putting it in individual packages for daily use. The personally prepared diet needed special seasonings, of course. Thus the

Baron ate like royalty from his second year on, or at least until he suffered some stomach upset that required a change in the diet. He received a very small dose of aspirin for some minor arthritis aches and it ripped his stomach badly, causing extensive bleeding. Thereafter his diet changed to baked chicken shreds, cottage cheese, and a small amount of dry dog food. He loved it and we were never able to get him back on his earlier diet.

I do not know if the Baron was pampered, but he did eat better than we did a great deal of the time. Buffy loved it when he was around at feeding time, he regarded it as a party rather than dinner.

+++

Baron loved cheese. It was highest on his list of the good things in life. I had never seen him drool until we were having cheese with dinner one evening. Normally he did not bother us while we were eating. He would just sit back and watch hoping for a treat. I was in the midst of eating a lovely piece of cheddar cheese when I realized our crazy dog was drooling. He never drooled.

142

I offered him a small piece and nearly lost my fingers. He was absolutely nuts about cheese. It was one of the few things that would cause him to break his self control. Cheddar was his favorite, but he had nothing against Edam, Swiss, goat, or blue cheese. What little training we were able to do with him was related to his love of cheese. We have it to thank for his response to sit, stay, and come commands. Heel was more than even cheese could accomplish.

Although I have kidded my wife about her pampering the Baron, the diet generated a healthy, 106 pound dog over a few years. It even produced a beautiful coat, including that on his rump. Of his many diets, the Bear liked the chicken, cottage cheese, and dry dog food the best. He ate it throughout his remaining years with us.

+++

Late in Baron's life he became incontinent. At my age I could understand the problem, but not the suggested solution. The vet wanted to castrate the old boy as one remedy. It helped, but did not completely eliminate the problem. We were at a loss about what to do when I discovered Depends, a diaper used by adults having the same problem. It seemed to us that we could design something in nighttime wear for the Baron.

It took some imaginative engineering, but we developed a night wear for him that worked. We split, or cut a hole in one end of the diaper for his tale, and then pulled the major portion of the garment under his belly up to his chest. This was held in place by three elastic strips that crossed his back and chest, and connected with the garment at his chest. It not only worked well, but Bear offered us no resistance to the night wear. When it was time, he would stand patiently while we put on his harness along with the diaper.

The "doggy diddy" simplified our life greatly, and we think Bear's as well. He wore it for the last year of his life. The only problem was that no one would believe that I was buying Depends for our dog. Merchants would just smile and say "sure you are." In the end it occurred to me that it was better that they thought it was me. I am sure that they would have thought a Depends wearing dog was, in reality, even more daft than my description. Only our vet thought it

144

a great idea and suggested it to other owners of older dogs having the same problem.

+++

Bear guaranteed that my wife and I walked more than we had ever done before. We walked through the park in the morning, the surrounding hills in the afternoon, and the Lawrence Hall of Science in the late afternoon where Buffy and the Bear would drink from the specimen pool at the back of the hall. On rare, but special, occasions the Bear and I walked the hiking trails by moonlight. For all of us, these were the best of times. We walked, dawdled over wild flowers, met other dogs, cats, people, and wild animals such as rabbits, coyotes, and deer. Once we even found the remains of a mountain lion's kill, but fortunately did not meet the lion. We took the time to look at a world and its simple pleasures, and it was Bear and his friend, Buffy, that helped us rediscover the nature that surrounded us. Even with death, Bear taught us something about grace and the joy of new life. Simple pleasures became magnified and unexpected delights filled our days.

Olli

Jenny

Spot

During Bear's tenure with us we lost Oliver, Jenny, Spot, and Buffy. All had lived full and long lives and although we missed them, we could not argue that they had not had their full share of good years. The pattern of change had brought us Boots, Holly, and Toby to dispel any sadness resulting from our other losses. Bear had taught us to accept the arrivals and departures of life with equanimity and understanding, a generous gift from a friend and faithful companion.

+++

Bear died suddenly as the result of a tragic accident. A neighbor at the end of the block had adopted a large, male Dalmatian a few years earlier. Mike, as he was called, was young, energetic, strong, and aggressive. Whenever we passed his house, he would charge the fence, or if locked in, the windows, barking and charging as if possessed by the devil himself. His owner had difficulty in controlling him, and did not understand Mike's behavior toward other animals. She thought he only wanted to play.

One day in May, 1994, Mike pulled away from his

146

Buffy

owner during their afternoon walk and charged the Bear and me. I had seen them coming down the street and had turned into a local children's park to get out of their way and sight. Unfortunately, Mike saw us and his owner did not. She was talking to a friend. He pulled his lead free from her hand and charged down the hill directly at Bear. I tried to intercede but was knocked down by Mike who also hit the Baron knocking him on down the hill. We both fell into a bed of ivy which may have tangled up the Barons right hind quarters. Before I could drive Mike off of the Bear we both rolled farther down the hill. When the owner finally arrived to restrain her dog, I discovered that the Bear could not rise. He tried valiantly to stand, but his right rear leg would not support him. It was obvious that his leg had been broken. I managed to get him down to a lower place that was level and lay him down. Nearby was a neighbor and his child who had been playing in the park; they agreed to watch the Baron while I ran home to get our car. It took me about fifteen minutes, but it seemed much longer before I could get back with transportation. There on the level spot I had found for the Bear sat the neighbor, his child, their dog Fritz, and the Bear, quietly and peacefully looking over the park as if nothing had happened. Bear was resting and enjoying the view with his new friends.

My wife and I got the old boy to our veterinarian who confirmed a major fracture just above the middle joint in the leg. Bear's size, and the location of the fracture, made it impossible to splint the leg in normal fashion. Surgical repair using metal plates was required. The good news was that it was operable, and in spite of his age, Bear was considered a good candidate for surgery. Unfortunately, during the operation, it was discovered that Bear's leg bones were soft and the metal screws holding the leg together were tenuous. Nevertheless, following surgery we took our friend home. A weekend intervened and we were to try and get Bear, with our support, to walk on the surgically repaired leg. He was simply too large for the two of us to handle by ourselves.

By Monday it was clear that he could not stand and that there were complications that no one had expected. Our vet stopped by the house and picked our friend up to transport him back to surgery for more X-rays. He had a new fracture that had occurred over the weekend at home. His bones were too soft to stand further surgery and there was nothing else that could be done for a dog his age and size. Amputation was out of the question, and it was clear that the fragile nature of the dog's bones could not tolerate additional intervention even if we thought it appropriate, which we did not. So we faced the question no one wants to consider for a faithful friend and companion, "Should we have him put to death?" We worried over the options for a couple of hours and then faced the fact that our choices were limited by his age, condition, and negative prognosis. He was in pain and could not get better.

He had lived a long life, fifteen or sixteen years we thought. Of those years he had lived eight with us in what we believed were good years. Although earlier than we hoped or expected, Bear's time had come. No matter how much we regretted it, we had but one choice left and that was to let him go painlessly, peacefully, and quietly. We made our decision with deep sorrow.

Before injecting Bear with everlasting sleep, we were able to spend time with him giving him his favorite treats, chicken and cheese. There was nothing he would not do for either and both made him drool with anticipation, something he did for us on his last afternoon. In pain, and not really hungry, he relished the treats and the petting and loving provided by all of the staff who knew him so well. He trusted these people who had looked after him and cared for him. And, he no longer turned his eyes away when we looked into them. Indeed, he had learned to look back with absolute trust and confidence into the souls of those he loved.

He left us with the assurance that Buffy, Jenny, Oliver, and Spotty, his friends, were waiting for him and that we would all once again run the trails in the park together. He died peacefully in our arms while we were loving him. His gaze never left ours until his eyes slowly closed. We hope that he understood our promises and our decision. For two old warriors like ourselves, it was one of the most difficult decisions that we ever made.

Buffy and the Bear

+++

Both Buffy and the Bear were special experiences that planned or not, greatly changed our lives and the way we look at the experiences we enjoy with the carnival of animals that surround us each day. We both received love and affection from our other animals, but not to the extent Buffy and the Bear offered each other and us. Their time was joyful and rewarding to all who had the pleasure of knowing them. We came to understand the concept of "faithful companion and friend" with a new clarity. It was an experience for which we are grateful, one we never will forget.

Still Friends

Boots, Holly, and the Mayor of Fairlawn Drive

One year to the month after Bear appeared on the doorstep, Boots arrived in the back garden among the raccoons, skunks, and possum. He was a dark gray tabby with white front paws and hind leggings. The markings were striking and immediately identified him as Mittens and Boots. He came each night to munch on the generic dog food left out for the wild ones. It was an amusing sight to see him struggle to chew the large nuggets, but he did, with great success. If we tried to approach him to offer a more manageable cat chow, he would withdraw a few feet, hiss, and make low guttural warning sounds. His behavior suggested he was a feral cat, but his appearance did not. He was short and stubby, had reasonably good conformation, and a thick coat of fur. If he was wild, his survival skills were very successful.

Unknown to us, Boots, as we now referred to him, had been sneaking into our living room through the cat door after the lights went out. He had found a place on the rug just in front and below the couch where Olli slept. When we finally discovered him he scurried out the cat door on the deck and disappeared into the dark until the lights went off. Then he would quietly sneak back in to the same place and curl up for the night. During all of this, Olli just watched; he never charged him or seemed disturbed by his presence. In old age, Number One had mellowed greatly and was willing to live and let live.

I suppose this arrangement would have gone on indefinitely if we had not taken a group of colleagues to China on a professional exchange. Our friend, who usually looked after the house for us when we were away, planned to go with us on this trip. Her parents were planning to visit from the East so she arranged for them to house sit for us and look after the animal kingdom. They did not understand that we had three cats inside, Jenny, Olli, and Spot, and one wild one out-

Jenny

Olli

Spot

side. Our friend's mother assumed that all four cats belonged to us and treated them accordingly. When we returned home three weeks later, the wild one had been tamed and was now a regular member of the house-hold. In fact, he had developed a strong attachment to Jenny and became a part of Queenie's royal retinue. Jenny was intolerant of Spot and would not let him near her. Yet, Boots followed her around the garden and spent long hours keeping her company in the late afternoon sunlight.

Although Boots was friendly, he was still cautious and ready to bolt if he thought he was cornered. He needed to be neutered, but we delayed because of his tentative acceptance of us. He came home one day with a series of wounds and battle scars that led to abscess-es so we captured him and took him to the veterinari-an for treatment. When we delivered him we had warned them that he might be a feral cat, that they should treat him carefully.

The next day we went to pick him up and return him home. He was curled up in a fuzzy pink circular bed, looking like a waif. On the cage door was a sign,

155

Boots

with big red letters, that read "WILD CAT." So much for the inadequacy of human language and our attempt to alert staff of a possible problem. His wounds had been treated, he had been neutered, and was ready to come home, but only if he took a number of pills for infection, and other possible complications. That afternoon we learned what kind of patient our new friend was—not good!

The Pill Spitter

We have never had an animal friend who liked to take medication. They all resist it one way or another. But, Boots was a champion resister. He had a tongue action that expelled any foreign substance introduced into his mouth. If his quick and sneaky tongue flick was not successful, he had a second remarkable line of defense: he was able to quietly hold a pill in his mouth for up to five minutes, not spitting it out until we had turned our backs. Boots was allergic to pollen, probably because he had no undercoat of fur. Since we did not want a bald cat every spring, we engaged in the

156

battle of the pills annually.

Boots arrival, as it turned out, was as a replacement for Olli who died while we were in China. Sad as his death was for us, particularly since it had occurred while we were away, Boot's presence made his departure easier. In some ways Olli's acceptance of Boots before we had left suggested that a very natural transfer had taken place.

Olli picked out his successor, and a good choice it turned out to be. His thoughtfulness in choosing his replacement softened the grief for all of us. Jenny had a replacement caring companion, who looked after her as if she were a litter mate. Whenever we missed her we would turn to Boots and tell him to "Go find Jenny." Soon she would appear, followed by her faithful new companion. Contrary to his early image as "a wild cat," Boots turned out to be one of the sweetest, even-tempered animals to live with us and join the carnival.

+++

"Roofs are safe."
Holly

Holly, who also came to us during this period, is quite another story. She was adopted by a neighbor at about the same time Boots arrived in our garden. Actually, our neighbor had adopted two cats, Mike and the one who we came to call Holly. Mike was a loving homebody, but Holly resisted attention and refused to stay around the house, be picked up, petted, etc. Our neighbor complained that she was not "a proper cat." Holly finally ran away from the neighbor's home, but not the general area. We would see her in an open garage up the street, on roof tops mewing for attention, and just roaming through yards across and up the street. No one figured out how to get near her. Approach her, even offer her food and she would flee. Long-haired, her fur became matted and she looked awful. She was thin and obviously not doing well on her own, but would not let anyone offer her help. Our next door neighbors were greatly concerned and decided that they had to do something to tame her down.

They began by putting dry food out on their back porch, but couldn't keep it there because Boots discovered this treasure and would go over and eat it all. So, they got two bowls to set on the porch, one for Boots and one for the strange one. Boots turned out to be valuable in the experiment. He did not bother the wild one, and indeed seemed to provide her with some reassurance. Within a couple of weeks they could be seen eating side by side whenever food was put out. Eventually our neighbors were able to open their kitchen door and talk to Boots, and in time even to the other one. But, make even a gesture in her direction and she was off into the night. In time she came to let our neighbor pet her, something she craved desperately. But again, to try and pick her up or restrain her and she freaked out, frantically running off to escape whatever horror she imagined.

The taming of the wild one took place slowly, and only because of the unbelievable patience of our neighbor. In time he could open the kitchen door without the cat taking flight. She would even step inside, but then quickly leave as well. Within a couple of months he could pick her up, and by not holding her tightly, pet her in his arms for short periods before letting her jump down. She had learned to trust him, just a little.

159

At about this time, our neighbors learned that the husband was to be transferred to the East Coast by the Army. He was concerned about his wild friend and what was going to happen to her. We volunteered to see if we could help her make the transition from their house to ours. We began by putting out the expected food at our back door while the neighbors reduced it at theirs. Boots was again the necessary factor in bringing about the change.

The outsider would follow Boots over to our house and peer longingly through the sliding glass doors at the food he was eating. But she would not come in. We moved the food just outside and soon Boots and the wild one were eating at our backdoor, generally before the wildlife arrived. She would still not come near us. As a result, we gradually moved the food inside. The wild one followed reluctantly and cautiously. I also began to spend time sitting on the bottom step to the garden. It took her almost a week to accept even this limited closeness. I made no gestures at touching or picking her up and just sat there so that she could, of her own free will, rub up against me and be petted when she was ready. In time, I could pick her up and hold her loosely while I petted her. She would purr loud enough to be heard from several feet away.

The process started next door worked, but very slowly. The wild one could learn to trust, but only tentatively. During this period we felt silly calling the cat the "Wild One." We decided that proper cat or not, she needed a name. Holly seemed appropriate and described her behavior. We named her after Holly Golightly, the character in Breakfast at Tiffany's, for she was indeed a genuine 100% flake, something that has not changed greatly over the years.

She loves and craves attention, but not control. Closed doors mean loss of control to her and it frightens her a great deal to be unexpectedly trapped. As a result, we try hard to keep at least one route of escape available whenever she is inside. With time and age she has gotten better, but still resists any form of unwanted control. You rarely hold her, and when you do it must be lightly so that she can go when she wants to go. Capture her when she doesn't expect it and she will disappear for the day when you finally release her. After all of the years she has been a part of the animal carnival, we still have no idea of what created the fear that still drives a great deal of her behavior. We have accepted the fact that she will always be our resident flake, one we love and accept, but do not understand.

+++

We were still in the process of trying to convince Holly that it was OK to come in the house when Jenny fell ill. At age eighteen she was not as sprightly as in her prime, but she was still bright-eyed, alert, and reigning as the queen of her domain. She showed no obvious symptoms of failing health and had passed her annual physical in the spring with flying colors. By Thanksgiving, her eating patterns had changed substantially and she was increasingly becoming lethargic. We took her to the veterinarian and he diagnosed kidney failure. He kept her for a couple of days to see if she would respond to treatment, but the years had taken their toll. We discussed her options, some of them pretty exotic, like a transplant. We all agreed that she had enjoyed a good, healthy life, (not withstanding the brief period with the obnoxious tenants), and it would not be right to subject our regal dowager to the indignities of radical interventions. Her vet assured us that she was not in pain, and that the time left would involve decreasing energy, followed by the possibility of a catatonic state that would last only a day or two before she died. We took her home to her chair and room with the classic radio station playing.

For two weeks Jenny did well and showed no signs of being anything but an old cat. Then one day she joined me in the study where I was working, lay down on her pillow, closed her eyes and quietly died while listening to a Brahm's violin concerto. She decided that a catatonic state was too theatrical. She was queenly in life and even regal in death.

Holly refused to enter the house while Jenny was alive. She would watch her through the sliding glass doors, and Jenny would watch her in return. On her last day, Jenny walked to the door very slowly and sniffed noses with Holly, their first physical encounter. It was as if she was telling Holly that it was time she stopped her wandering and came in to live with Boots, and so it was that Jenny chose her successor. Holly came in, but not until the day after Jenny's death.

+++

Holly is a tortoise seal point with long, thick, silky fur. She is cream and seal brown in color with flashes of tan on her face, and her eyes are sky blue. She is a handsome cat, and all things considered, a worthy addition to the carnival on the hill, even if she is a flake. When settled on the bed or in one of her favorite chairs, you can pet her, sometimes pick her up, lavish her with attention, if she wants it, but only if she feels she can escape.

Boots and Holly had become inseparable companions, just as Boots and Jenny had. Where one went the other followed. There is no question that Holly was smitten with Boots, and he was tolerant of her attention. When he appeared she would run up to him, rub against him, and give him a couple of friendly licks. He did his best to ignore the whole thing, but then, he never did resist in any aggressive way. In retrospect, it occurs to me that neither my neighbor nor I tamed Holly; it was Boots.

164

Inseparable
companions

+++

Just before Holly moved in we met Toby. Our neighbor across the street brought him home as a kitten. He was a buff-colored rumpy manx. Friendly and inquisitive, he would visit us daily for a snack and playtime with various cat toys and Boots' tail. But he only visited, and regularly returned home to eat and sleep in a large green chair in his living room. Our neighbor was an invalid, and had a live-in caretaker. The two spoiled Toby rotten with attention. He was pampered and loved every bit of it. Our neighbor knew Toby spent considerable time with us and approved of it since she knew that he might one day need a new home. That day came within a year when our neighbor died and we were asked if we would like to have Toby. We quickly responded yes and Toby became a new member of our household on a permanent basis. He was not at all sure that we were an acceptable substitute, however. In his former home he was the only pet and was always the center of attention. Now he was faced with the prospect of sharing his new domain with other cats, and the Baron. He knew them all, but had not planned on living with them in their mixed community. Before, he

165

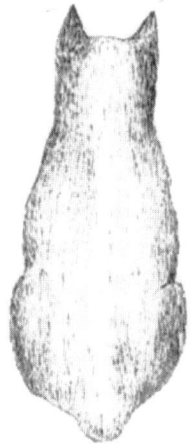

Toby

could take them or leave them at his option.

His move across the street was only a short distance, but a much longer journey of the will for Toby. The transition was not easy for him. He was a free spirit and had roamed the entire neighborhood at his convenience and interest. He was known by everyone as the cat without a tail or "The Mayor of Fairlawn Drive," because he enjoyed meeting everyone and everything coming along the road.

Boots

His move was made difficult by the presence of the other animals, but also by the different activities of the people who lived in his new house. Having to compete for space in his new home made him wander even farther than he had previously gone. Away most of the day he would only return late at night to eat and sleep in a large red chair in the living room. He was just beginning to settle in when we lost the Baron. The house fell into a shambles and all of the animals seemed to sense the change in our lives. Boots and Holly still had each other, but Toby was the odd cat out. He began wandering in earnest, gone for days at a time. On one of our walks we found him several blocks

Holly

Toby

away from the house in another neighborhood. We carried him home, but only to have him leave again.

We began posting "Toby Alerts" throughout the immediate and extended neighborhoods. The alerts became legend because of their frequency. The alerts identified Toby, listed our address and phone number, and asked people to love and pet him, but not feed him since he had a home. Toby sightings were frequent, and we learned the names of a lot of our neighbors. Sightings of the mad manx or tailless cat were reported all over the hill on a regular basis by a helpful community. In desperation we decided that we had to adopt some strategy to convince him that he had a home and was expected to spend at least some time with us to reassure us if nothing more. He had been left in our trust and we intended to keep it.

My wife was the first to recognize that we had to provide Toby with some space that he could identify as his own—a place where the other animals did not go. We had a basement room that met these specifications. My wife decided that this was to be Toby's sanctuary. She didn't explain that I was to be exiled there as well during his transition. We began the experiment by taking him down in the early evening and keeping him inside until bedtime when the couch became a bed which he and I shared. He also had his own litter box, water bowl, and food container.

Initially, Toby argued with me about the merits of being released from his retreat, but eventually came to accept the routine, but not without kneading once I was under the covers. He would creep up somewhere near my neck and then begin a routine that would go on for some time. It was as if I was a surrogate mother or something. He would finally exhaust himself before curling up for the night. We then slept uninterrupted until first light, at which time Toby advised me that it was time to let him escape to his world of adventure. Off he would go until the late afternoon when he would return home for dinner and the peace of his private basement room.

It took almost two weeks for him to accept the fact that he now lived in a new home. He even began to accept staying with the whole gang upstairs and watch the evening parade of raccoons, possum, and skunks. He was willing to fight for his place on the couch, at the backdoor for the passing parade, or wherever. His assurance grew, and he accepted both Boots and Holly as if they were litter mates.

Although he no longer sleeps there, the downstairs room continues to be his special place. The door cannot be opened without his hearing it and appearing on the spot immediately. He spends time checking the room out, sitting in a chair keeping us company for awhile, and then leaving once he knows that his room is still there. It is still his room, his retreat, and place of solace.

Toby is very people-oriented, gentle, and loves attention. He also hates competition with other animals and avoids it if at all possible. As the Mayor of Fairlawn Drive he still visits his many friends, people and animals. He will walk up to an absolute stranger and lean into him or her to be stroked. Even though most neighbors know him, strangers wonder aloud about "what happened to his tail?" He also finds high ground on various fences where he talks to passersby about his many adventures.

169

Red

A Tale of
many tails

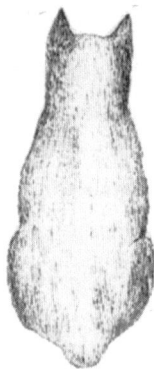

Toby is fascinated with tails. He spent endless time examining Boots and Holly's tails trying to understand why they had them and he did not. He is also interested in the tails of Floppy and Red, two squirrels who frequent our garden and get peanuts as their reward. His interest is unending, as is his energetic pursuit of his two red friends. Neither of them take him seriously, but they do enjoy scolding him for interfering with their collection of peanuts. His greatest obsession, much to our concern, is a small young skunk called Gorgeous. She has a magnificent tail, a thing of beauty to Toby, and will be until he learns the negative reality of that tail. We keep our fingers crossed and the doors and windows closed when he is in pursuit of this newfound beauty. Oh yes, we also keep the V8 Juice stocked just in case.

Fate paid my wife back for abandoning Toby and I to the basement room. After we both moved back upstairs, Toby decided that my wife was a much better knead than I was and turned his attention to her. At first she tried to shield herself from the attention with blankets, but finally recognized that a heavy sweat shirt would be better. He transferred his annoying loyalties

171

quickly, much to my pleasure, and my wife still has to play the role of his surrogate mother when he feels the need for a good knead. Justice prevailed.

+++

We lost Boots a few years after Toby's arrival. During his annual physical examination a large tumor was discovered on his spleen. It appeared operable since he seemed in good health and because of his age. Unfortunately, the tumor had already spread to other organs and Boots died in surgery.

We all felt the loss, but no one more than Holly who had lost her mentor, friend, and playmate. The carnival was getting older and smaller in number, but its joy and pleasure persists for those of us taking time to watch and enjoy the antics of our animal friends. We never know who will join us next.

The Carnival Continues

A year after the Baron died the carnival returned to a familiar collection of cats, innumerable raccoons, skunks, deer, and jay birds who competed with the squirrels for peanuts and generic dog food left over from the previous night's feeding of raccoons. In spite of the heavy loss we felt with Bear's absence we were again recognizing that the circle of life goes on, and we are blessed with a never-ending series of new friends who entertain and delight us with the coming of each day. Some remain to keep us company, and others are only temporary visitors.

+++

During the Baron's early days with us we became aware of an increasing number of deer visiting our garden regularly. Although Bear had been known to chase

a deer in the park, he never made a threatening gesture at any of those visiting our garden. He would watch them from the dining room, but he would never bark or startle them, only look on quietly as they ate whatever satisfied their tastes from our plants.

Before we had gone to Washington D.C., we had seen an occasional buck or doe pass through the garden, but never spend long, regular hours with us. We attributed the changes in patterns of behavior to the maturing of the vegetation, a drought, and an increasing deer population in the park. Originally, the garden had been sparsely vegetated, but as our interest changed, so too had the garden. What had been open space was thick with shrubs, plants, and trees. One area in particular was made into a leaf dump for mulch. The deer had discovered it and found it soft, cool, and private. As a result, we frequently had visitors who would spend the entire day with us in their chosen part of the garden. The cats and dog accepted them as they do all of our other visitors, with tolerance and no recognizable concern.

Fortunately, we have several plants that lend themselves to being deer snacks and thrive on the natural trim. Others do not always fare so well. The deer come and munch, stay and rest, and share our space and time with equanimity. Each year the does bring their offspring to the garden, which is a delight to see. While some of the plants are trimmed closer than we might like, the overall balance between plants and animals is acceptable.

+++

We are responsible for encouraging the passing carnival and therefore are responsible for all of the obligations that go with inviting animals, wild or otherwise, to share our space. Unfortunately, we sometimes unwittingly fail in this obligation. A few years ago, one of the does we had come to know began her regular visits to the leaf mulch area of the garden. She brought her two new fawns. They were tiny and still spotted. A few days after her arrival, she came crashing down into the patio, falling about four feet. Somewhere above our house she had become entangled in a steel wire plant protector, shaped like a giant cone. Her head was caught in the smaller portion of the

175

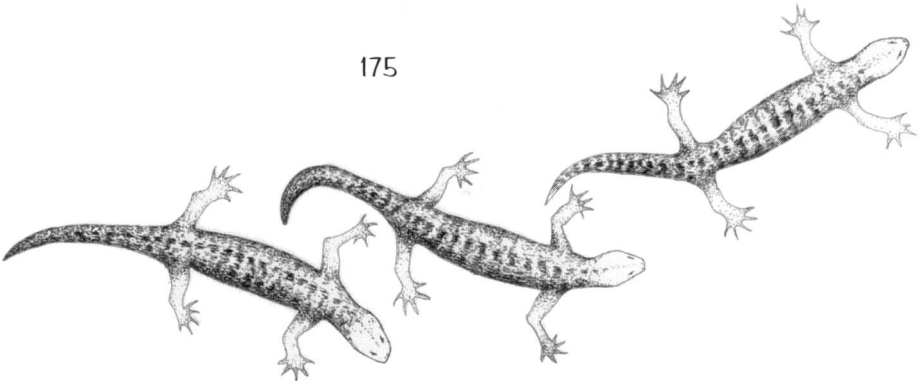

wire frame and a foot in the larger open circle on the other end. The wire was cutting into her neck, and I could see no way that she was going to get out of the predicament without assistance. She was frightened, hobbled, and seriously cut by the wire. There was nothing we could do without skilled help.

I began by calling our local animal control. They advised me that large animals were not their problem unless dead. They offered no suggestions. I then called Tilden Regional Park Headquarters since the animal had come from the park. I was informed that it was not their problem until the animal came back into the park, but they did have an idea. The Department of Agriculture had wardens who devoted their time to animal problems like this one. They offered to call and have someone contact me. They did shortly, agreeing to have someone at the house within an hour. During the many telephone calls, the doe and fawns stayed in the garden for sometime before slowly disappearing up the animal trail en route to the park. Sadly, when we last saw her, she was still hobbled and entangled in the steel wire plant protector. She moved very slowly, to avoid falling.

176

When the warden arrived and we explained the problem, particularly our concern for the two small fawns, and the probability that the wire, still entangled around the doe's neck and feet, would not come off without help. We told the warden that we believed the doe and fawns were making their way back to the park and offered her a way to confirm it. A neighbor's garden overlooks the animal trail about 200 yards down a ravine from our garden. We took the game warden down to the neighbor's yard where, with her field glasses, she could see the doe, still entangled with the wire, having great trouble walking. She too thought the doe was in danger, but was not sure that she could offer much help. They had a tranquilizer gun and darts, but it was several miles away in another county. She wasn't sure it would work in any event. Once hit, the animal would try and run, exacerbating her problem. However, a U.C. Berkeley professor had been studying the deer population in the park and had used collapsing cages that might be an answer. She agreed to contact him. The following day we had three game wardens and a university professor gathered in our garden, setting up a collapsing deer trap. It was made up of a series of connected pipes and a large mesh webbing that controlled, but did not injure the animal. Everyone was getting into the rescue operation. The trap was baited with rotten fruit, something we were told that the deer could not resist. In theory, the deer walked into the trap after the fruit, tripped a trigger, and dropped a gate. When help arrived, the trap would be collapsed on the deer for control, the wire cut off, and the deer released. Unfortunately, the size of the garden created several problems. There was not really enough room for the trap or the deer's later escape if our plan worked.

The experts admonished us that regardless of familiarity with the animal, the doe was a wild animal that would, when trapped, go berserk in her terror at being trapped. If terrorized, she would be likely to make loud screaming sounds. Under no circumstances were we to collapse or open the trap without their help. We were also scolded about feeding the wildlife and contributing to overpopulating the area around the garden. What could I say? They were right. We had spent the greater part of fifty years encouraging and supporting the wild things that live near us. It was a natural thing for us to do.

178

The Carnival Continues

The first night I had to go out and reset the trap three times. The raccoons and all of their friends had gathered en mass to enjoy the rotting fruit. None went in, they just reached in through the large openings in the string mesh that made up the trap, grabbed the fruit and sat back to enjoy it. The strategy of the animals to avoid the open cage door worked, but reaching through the mesh kept setting off the trap. We have had lots of animals in the garden, but not in the numbers that showed up then. The second night was almost an exact replay except the deer, a companion, and the fawns also arrived. They would not go near the trap, except to circle it. Supporting ropes were strung out in four directions, and the still-hobbled doe kept stumbling over her wire restraint. Once she tripped and almost fell off of the retaining wall on me, a potential disaster since she weighed close to 175 pounds.

The two nights' experience strongly suggested that we were in a losing game and that the deer faced greater injury from our well-intentioned efforts than if left alone. I called the game wardens and told them our assessment. They agreed and came by the next day to pick up the trap and again tell me to stop feeding the

179

wild animals. I felt guilty at contributing to the problem, and even more so because of my inability to offer real help to the poor doe. Yet there was nothing more I could do except wait and expect the worst.

My neighbor to the north has a garden that parallels and overlooks the animal trail. His dining room windows have a clear view of the path for several hundred yards. Two days after the trap was removed he spotted the doe and fawns walking along the trail. She appeared to be free of the wire tangle. I immediately went down to see if he was correct. Using my field glasses I was able to confirm the fact that the wire was gone. Somehow, she had freed herself of the plant protector, and was walking normally. We had several visits from the doe and her offspring later that year, and none revealed that she was worse off from the experience. They spent many undisturbed hours in the nest of leaves, free of wardens, well-intended residents, and traps.

The Carnival Continues

Two other stories come to mind where intervention helped. One spring, my wife kept hearing the "chittering" of baby raccoons. They went on all day and all night. After two nights, we decided to locate them. Next door there was an old compost box that had been there for years. On our side of the box was an opening of about six by twelve inches. Looking out were three small raccoon kittens. I lifted the lid of the box and discovered five kittens, all chittering in hunger and fright. My wife and I agreed to keep an eye on them for a couple of days, and if there was no sign of the mother returning we would intervene.

We waited the two days, and found that the five kittens were now three. We had no way of knowing what had happened to the two missing kittens, but suspected that hunger had driven them to search for their mother, and eventually they were killed or died of starvation. The three remaining kittens were no longer active or even threatening. They simply lay curled up together hungry and in frightened silence. I put on my leather gloves, since even kittens have sharp teeth and claws, and placed them in a towel lined box to take to the Lindsay Wildlife Museum, in Walnut Creek. The kittens were malnourished, infested with fleas, and almost catatonic. We learned that one was not strong enough to survive. The other two were kept for several months of treatment and rehabilitation before being released to their natural habitat.

The museum is a pleasant, small facility that provides the opportunity for children and adults to learn up close about wild animals native to the area. It also operates a hospital and treatment program for injured native wildlife. It is supported by charitable contributions from the community, either for educational programs offered by the museum or for injured animals they treat. It is a remarkable museum and service to the community.

A few years later we had a second experience that led to our use of the Lindsay program. Again, my wife heard a chittering from a raccoon kitten. She found the little critter hanging from a tree, caught in deer netting, a miserable thin nylon threaded material that catches birds and animals in its web and can severely injure them. The kitten was not about to be picked up or lifted to be set free. The webbing was tightly entangled around the toes of his left hind paw. There was no way we could free the animal without its being immobilized. I made a couple of feeble attempts to subdue the little devil, but without success. It was frightened, angry, and even though tiny, ready to defend herself against anyone. She was a fury mass of teeth and claws waiting to cut into the flesh of anyone trying to help. We got out the cat box, opened the door, and carefully began cutting the netting from around our friend. I held the netting tight as I cut it, stretching the kitten out from the bound hind leg. She went reluctantly into the cat box, head first, and only after several aborted tries, and several near misses from fang and claw to the rescuers. Once again, we were reminded that, familiar or not, small or not, our friend was a wild animal and deserved the cautious and careful handling that her wild status demands.

The Lindsay staff advised us that we had captured a female raccoon who had cut off some of her toes in her struggle for freedom. Her injuries were severe enough to require extended treatment before she could be released. She was accepted for care without obligation, hospitalized for two months, and then conditioned for release in a large wild compound for another sixty days before being released back into her natural habitat. The Lindsay had again come to our rescue. On two occasions, we had been able to get our wild friends the help they needed when they needed it, something for which we are deeply grateful.

+++

We like to think that there is some understanding among all of the local animals that our garden and house are safe for all creatures, great and small, although we began to think that we might make an exception for one raccoon.

A few years ago, a small, female raccoon began visiting us in the late afternoon, never at night as did all of the others. She was a delight, and we named her Tinkerbelle. She was tame, friendly, but obviously at war with other raccoons. At times she would appear with gaping wounds, but she was a survivor. She produced several litters of kittens before departing the scene. We are convinced that one of her progeny is a current visitor who is driving us crazy.

Slippery was given that name because she is crafty, and as devious as anything we have ever experienced from wildlife. She is small, fearless, and imaginative with an apparent perverse sense of humor. She comes alone and acts as if this is her house to be entered at will. She quickly learned that by climbing a weeping cherry tree she could make her way onto the deck, slip through a sliding glass door on the deck, left open for the cats, and dine on the delectable cat chow she found in the kitchen.

We could not have her coming and going to suit her will so we put dead bolts on the doors and reduced the glass door opening to only three inches in width. Obviously, it was too small for a raccoon to squeeze through—we thought. The opening was barely large enough for a cat's head, let alone a raccoon. Slippery studied the obstacle for a week before determining that although she could not come through the door head first, she could stand up, clasp her paws around the door jam and shimmy through the opening side-ways. Although we found telltale paw marks on the wall, we could not figure out how she was getting in until I saw her in the act.

We experimented with other ways to block the narrow opening without success. Obviously, the solution was to prevent her from climbing the tree up to the deck. But, how would we do that without cutting down the tree? First, we tried a large, plastic veterinarian collar around the trunk at the top of the tree. The collar slowed her down for one night. She showed up in the house again, and finding no food on the floor, spent her time playing with and devouring two catnip mice and a souvenir beanbag frog from Puerto Rico.

My wife and I both remembered that zoos prevent animals from clawing and climbing trees by encasing the base with aluminum metal. The next day I was given the task of wrapping the trunk of the cherry tree in heavy gage aluminum up to the plastic collar. Now she could not climb the tree. We felt sorry for the poor animal; we had beaten her—or so we thought.

Within two nights, Slippery was back at the cat food in the kitchen. We had placed it on the sink, but that did-

n't stop our determined raccoon. She climbed the draw-
er handles up to the sink. This was ridiculous; there was
no way she could have climbed the tree. She hadn't. She
had climbed the vertical wall parallel to the tree. The wall
juts out from the main frame of the house by about three
feet, enabling Slippery to put her front paws on either
side of the wall and shimmy up, much the same way as
she had with the tree. I then built a T-shaped barrier at
the top of the wall that she could not climb over. A part
of the three-foot barrier blocked access to the top of the
deck and the lower portion blocked access to the vertical
wall. We both agreed, there was no way a raccoon could
climb that wall now. Once again we declared victory and
opened a bottle of wine to celebrate.

We are both convinced that Slippery lay in wait,
watching our feeble antics to outwit her. Less than a
week after installing the fool-proof overhang, we were
awakened by a loud thud on the roof. Slippery was
back. She had climbed a tree in the back of the house,
walked out on a limb and dropped down to the roof
where she made her way across to the forty-five degree
angle wall that leads to the deck—the wall of the
Jennipoo slide. Slippery did not come down side saddle,

but at a run, and departed the same way. She was back.

We were both about to declare Slippery the victor when it occurred to me that inserting a panel in the narrow space leaving an opening at the bottom might solve the problem. It would prevent Slippery from standing up and slipping through sideways. After a number of trials and errors, I finally managed to construct a barrier for the door that left an opening only about three inches wide and eight inches high, enough space for a cat, but not for any raccoon, including Slippery. There was no longer any way that she could squeeze through the opening sideways.

Several weeks have gone by without finding our resourceful friend in the kitchen. The new barrier has seemed to work. She is still trying, however. She will come up to the insert and pull at it. She stays until I show up with a flashlight to investigate, at which time she puts her nose in the door as if to bait me. This time, however, we have not declared victory, only a truce with our friend. She did not gain the name of Slippery for nothing.

The Carnival Continues

+++

During the "Slippery Wars" there was a new arrival on the scene. We thought he was just passing by, but, like so many of our other friends, he was surveying the scene for his retirement plan. Completely black, short-haired, and laid back, this lean and lank cat showed up in the garden. He was not pushy, just observant. He watched the other cats cautiously but without any aggressive movements. He never challenged them, never intruded, just observed. He watched for three days before marching down the steps from the garden into the dining room, greeting us with a soft meow, and making himself at home on the couch in the living room. Thereafter he became a shadow, a second skin, who would not let either my wife or me out of his sight. We would throw him out the back door, close it and turn around to discover that he had made his way around the house, up over the deck and back into the living room. During his first couple of weeks with us he was always talking in his soft cat voice. The other cats accepted him, but reluctantly. He changed the balance of relationships that existed between Holly, Toby, and Boots, who was still with us. Toby seemed the most

Misto deciding to adopt us

accepting of the stranger and, on occasion, engaged in running play with the new cat. His behavior was playful like a kitten, and he was gentle with people and other animals. He obviously was someone's pet. We notified the local animal shelters, looked through the newspapers, and read neighborhood postings about lost cats. After a couple of weeks, if he was going to stay, we had to take him in for a physical examination. That was when we discovered that he had a special way to get even for anyone taking him to the vets. He got car sick. He threw up and defecated anytime we drove him to the vets. He never failed in all the time he was with us. The veterinarian staff were always ready to assist in helping us clean the cat up the moment we arrived, but we were on our own when we returned home.

+++

Our veterinarian advised us that our new friend was a seven or eight-year-old neutered male who had been on his own for some time. In addition to shots, his teeth needed cleaning and several of them extracted. The vet wisely suggested that we do a blood panel on the stranger to see if there was any reason why we should not keep him with our other animals. The results were mixed. His kidney and liver were functioning well, his thyroid was borderline, but he was a carrier of a feline immune deficiency virus. Transmitted by blood and sex, similar to HIV, he could pose a problem for our other animals. We considered the pros and cons and decided, based on this cat's docile behavior and his being castrated, that the risk to our other cats was minimal. But, his virus made him more susceptible to illness than our other animals.

We were presented with a lovable animal in need of a home but who was probably unadoptable if placed in a shelter. Given the options of destruction or abandonment, we elected to add another retiree to our household.

Mr. Mistoffelees, a name borrowed from T.S. Eliot's Book of Practical Cats, became an official addition to the carnival on the hill. We quickly learned that we had made a good choice. He turned out to be a sweetheart, and, we believe, a reincarnation of Spot. Besides having fewer teeth, he was forever wanting attention from people. He seemed to love everybody and everything. Like

Spot, he knew that love given is returned many-fold.

Misto, as he quickly became known, enjoyed his retirement with Boots, Holly, and Toby. Holly, took him under her wing, even trying to get him to play.

Misto stayed with us for several years before his illness prevailed and took him. But, before he left the carnival, he discovered the gastronomic joy of calamari, a sure sign that he was the reincarnation of Spot. His time with us was memorable, not only for his gentleness, but most of all because of his joy of life. Several times during his final year we thought it might be time for him to be put to sleep, but each time, his willpower kicked in and he would come back to us with a vitality that amazed everyone that knew him. During his last three months, we had to resort to injections of fluids to hydrate him. He would sit quietly on the kitchen sink unflinching while I injected the needle to add 200 cc of fluid between his shoulders. Then, as if by magic, he would perk up and join the other cats in their regular activities.

His tolerance of treatment and his love of life were

Misto

amazing to witness. Being a part of it was special, as was Misto. Finally, his illness became too strong for even him to resist, and he succumbed to a general failure of all his systems, quietly and peacefully. We had never before witnessed such a strong drive to keep living in any animal friend. He loved life and struggled gallantly to honor that love up to and including his final minutes. Dylan Thomas would have been proud. Misto did "not go gentle into that good night," but he did die with grace and style, just as he had lived.

+++

Several years ago my mother-in-law adopted a neighborhood calico cat, whose owners were leaving Southern California and could not take her with them. Although Maggie settled into her new home with ease, she always maintained a certain distance. It was not until she had mellowed with age that she allowed my mother-in-law to hold her. Yet, she was, for my in-laws, a welcome addition that kept them company for many years.

About a year after Maggie died, a new cat arrived

on their scene. A stray, she had been living under the house next door and had become trapped. She was friendly and approachable, and, with very little encouragement, became a member of my inlaws' household. She was marmalade colored with short, soft fur, and a long, full tail, not unlike that of a snow leopard. Christened Samantha, she was also known as Sam or Sammy. She was a perfect addition to the household of a couple in their nineties. From the beginning, she had an uncanny sense about being around elderly people. We observed that she would keep her eyes on their feet and quietly move away if they came too close so as to avoid tripping them or being stepped on.

Clearly Sammy belonged to my mother-in-law while she was alive, following her around and sitting next to her in her favorite chair. When she died, Sammy shifted her loyalty to my father-in-law. Not known as a cat fancier, he was soon won over and often proclaimed, "That cat is almost human." She provided companionship and comfort to both in their final years, following my mother-in-law for short walks down the street, and my father-in-law as he roamed the back yard counting his tomatoes. During the day, she respected their space, staying close but not in their way. Nighttime was another matter. Once they retired and the lights were out, the large house became her private domain where she raced from one room to the other until she too was ready to retire. Quiet prevailed until the dawn's early light when Sammy would resume her race with herself. Once her people got up, decorum returned.

When my father-in-law followed his wife in death, we were confronted with what to do with a Southern California cat, a "valley girl" as we liked to call her— young, spoiled, and a sun worshiper. We could not abandon her to an unknown future, so we decided to bring her north.

She traveled very well, causing no bother during the nine hour drive. Once in Berkeley, we placed her in a room that had been prepared for her, with her own sand box, eating and water dishes, and mouse toys. She settled into her new space without argument or disturbance. Our plan was to keep her isolated for about a week to let Toby and Holly hear her and even sniff her under the door. That was to be followed by supervised visits through the rest of the house, and eventually, freedom to roam the Berkeley hills.

Sammy precipitated a major crisis on her second day in her new house. I went into her room to check her food and water dish and found the room empty. There was no way she could have got out, yet she had disappeared. My wife and I felt anger, fear, guilt, and anguish at one point or another in our search for the missing cat. We systematically searched the room together, but without success. We expanded the search to the rest of the house with the same result. We then carefully surveyed the outside with one of us going up the street and one down, calling and hoping for a miracle. None was to be offered, and we returned home distrought at our carelessness and the loss of our feline inheritance. It was a bad day indeed; we both felt miserable.

At ten o'clock that evening, I thought I heard some-thing in the study where Sam had been placed. I turned on the light, and there sat Sammy, bright-eyed and ready for dinner. I felt relief and anger at her all at the same time. Her reappearance was impossible, yet there she sat as if nothing had happened, and for her, it had not. The next morning, we were still trying to figure out where she had hidden. The room we had her in is only about ten feet square. It contains a desk, computer, printer, two cabinets and a chair. There is absolutely no place Sam could have hidden, yet she had.

The following morning when I checked the room for Sammy, the darn cat was gone again. We repeated our previous search with the same result. Sammy was not in the room. This time, however, we accepted the fact that she was hiding, and it was not our responsibility to find her. She would appear when she was ready. Nevertheless, we made one more search and then gave up the effort as pointless. I took up my work for the day and had been at it for less than an hour when my wife came in to ask me something. While she was standing behind me, she touched my shoulder and pointed to two black file boxes stacked in the corner. I used them for the storage of manuscripts, working papers, etc. Both were filled to the top, or so I thought. The bottom box had some papers stacked about halfway to the top, with a small space in the back. In that space were two yellow eyes surrounded by a hunk of orange fur that revealed a private, dark little nest.

Sammy's Retreat

That black storage box, behind old manuscripts, remained her retreat for the next several days. Once comfortable with her new environment, Sam began to venture out, no longer needing a secret retreat. In her flight from fright Sammy turned her energies inward to peace, warmth, and isolation, while dealing with the uncertainties facing her in her new home. It worked for her, and was, with hindsight, a revealing experience for us about our behavior.

When Sammy was introduced to the rest of the house, she came face to face with Toby and Holly. We were most concerned about what the relationship would be between her and Holly as two competing females. This issue was settled immediately. As she approached Holly, Holly let forth with a low steady hiss as if to say, "I am Number One!" Sammy got the message. She has become territorial, however, zeroing in on poor Toby. He is now the center of her attention. She will follow him all over the house, getting as close as she can. Sometimes she settles for a stare down, but more often than not she charges him. He has been amazingly tolerant and has not turned on her, but I fear the time is coming when he will set the record straight

The Carnival Continues

about who was here first. Although taking longer than expected, the three cats seem to be getting used to each other. We are leaving it to them to work it out; we have done all we can to help in the transition.

Her first day outside was quite an adventure. After carefully investigating her own back yard, she ventured next door, and came face to face with a doe and buck. She froze and then beat a hasty retreat to "her room." Her wide-eyed expression seemed to say, "There are great big dogs out there. And one of them has horns!"

Sammy has become a welcome addition to our family. She is friendly, talkative, and as my father-in-law was so fond of saying, almost human. Like Jenny before her, she appreciates classical music. We keep the FM station on most of the day to keep her company. Although she now has the run of the house, she spends a great deal of her time with me in the study. She sits by the window for hours, looking out to the back garden and discovering critters she had probably never seen in Southern California: raccoons, possum, skunks, and squirrels. She is also fascinated with the blue jays that scold her in the garden. They are a

source of never-ending interest and fright to her. These demons from hell unmercifully dive and attack Sammy when she is sitting on the retaining wall watching them collect the peanuts we have put out for the squirrels. Yes Sammy, you are a long way from Southern California, and the life style you once knew. As a new member of the carnival, Sammy has yet to fully find her place, but she will, as have all of those who preceded her.

+++

The Carnival of Animals has attracted many different characters over the years, including some rare ones. Early in our life on the hill we met Ricky the mongoose, that I initially believed to be a wild weasel, but later discovered was a family pet living just up the hill from us. Everyone seemed to know him except us.

Our latest encounter has been with a coyote, a sly, shy, intelligent animal that we did not expect to meet, but did, even though fleetingly. We were tempted to call him Wile E. Coyote, after the cartoon character, but we decided he deserved a proper name that captures the

202

"I don't think this is
Southern California."

The Carnival Continues

dignity he shows, so we have dubbed him El Señor Coyote.

Señor Coyote first showed himself to us about two years ago late at night. We heard a commotion among the raccoons sharing generic dog food. The movement sensor lights came on, and there amidst five large raccoons, stood the saddest looking specimen of canine that we had ever seen. His fur was matted and falling off in great clumps. We debated about the poor animal, my wife insisting it was a fox, and I thought him a miserable dog, albeit a bit weird in body conformation and hair color, which was beige, brown, and scruffy looking. He had a large head with a pointed muzzle, pointed, bushy ears that stood upright, a thin body, four skinny legs, and a tail that was a shadow of his once proud plume. He was about twenty-five inches at the shoulder, and probably weighed only about thirty-five pounds in his starved condition. He certainly was not a fox, and if he was a dog, he was one of the strangest ones we had ever seen. He even looked stranger standing there amid the raccoons, all almost as big as he was.

He looked as if he was about to bolt from the scene,

Señor Coyote comes to dinner

but the lure of the generic dog food was too much for him to ignore. He munched on. He stood his ground and took his turn with the raccoons helping himself to mouthfuls of kibble. After the initial excitement, the raccoons accepted him as just another visitor to the carnival. We didn't see him again for several months, although from some of the sounds coming from the dark, we suspected that he was one of the many night visitors that come in the early hours of the morning.

We argued about his species for some time before calling the naturalist at Tilden Regional Park. She told us that from our description we had seen a coyote. I protested that coyotes were plains animals, and did not live in the hills. She kindly informed me that my knowledge was incorrect and that coyotes covered a much wider range than the great American plains. She suggested that I come by and take one of their pamphlets that describe wild animals to be found in Tilden Regional Park.

The pamphlet informed me that the coyote (Canis latrans, "barking dog") is cousin to the domestic dog and the wolf. He is native to the prairies, but circumstances have allowed him to extend his range from

Southern Canada to Central America. He is known to be cunning, has a "sense of humor," and the determination to survive wherever he finds himself—including in the Berkeley hills.

The coyote's habits depend largely on climate and habitat. They adapt. In Berkeley's temperate climate it would not be unusual for Señor Coyote to forage during daylight hours, unless harassed by humans. Coyotes do not share the pack hierarchy of wolves, tending to be solitary animals, which accounts for the singular sighting we have had. It also explains why they are not a danger to larger prey like large dogs, deer, or man, and why already dead animals are a large part of their diet.

After the original sighting we seldom saw Señor Coyote even though we thought we heard him barking and howling late at night. Then, one afternoon, quite recently, there was Señor Coyote in our back garden. I had just put out some generic dog food for one of our regular raccoons accompanied by her five, small, nursing kittens. She had become extremely agitated, scattered the kittens to nearby trees, then fixated on the garden opposite from where she was standing.

The Carnival Continues

Growling, she stood her ground and watched as our new friend once again made himself known, without being aggressive to the raccoon or her offspring. He looked no healthier than the last time we had seen him. He had gained a few pounds, but was not doing as well as we would have wished. Still wary and ready to bolt away, he permitted us to observe him from the kitchen, and even talk to him. He was thin, scruffy, and injured, with large chunks of fur coming off. It reminded us of how difficult survival was for some, even in Berkeley.

He finished his early evening snack and took off back up the hill to the animal trail. I wondered whether he was headed to the park or just somewhere else to finish his evening dinner. The trail follows the sewer easement at the back of the lot. In earlier days, before people had built decks and hot tubs, the trail was unobstructed and led down a ravine toward another street lower on the hill before turning back up the hill toward the park. Deer, possum, raccoons, dogs, cats, squirrels, etc. regularly make their way along this trail from house to house, and house to park. As I looked down at the trail, there went Señor Coyote. I thought he was headed for the park, but then he stopped, looked carefully about, and disappeared into the berry bushes. I thought no more about it until later that night when I remembered the old test mine shaft located along the trail. Maybe that's his den, and maybe that's the reason why he is still around the house.

The next morning I took my usual walk and was on the final leg coming up the hill when I saw a medium-sized dog up ahead of me. I spoke quietly to him to let him know he was being followed. He glanced over his shoulder, gave me a disinterested look and began to lope ahead just a bit faster. His new gait made me aware that I was not watching a dog, but Señor Coyote. He made his way on up the hill, around the turn, and disappeared between the houses that led back to the animal trail. He hadn't seemed frightened by my sudden appearance, but he was wary and not interested in socializing with this strange man that was following him.

Upon my arrival home, I told my wife that Señor Coyote and I had met once more. We both agreed that he too is a welcome addition to the carnival, since he is obviously in need of friends. If our suspicions are correct, and his den is in the old experimental mine shaft,

The Carnival Continues

I am sure we will soon see him again; at least I hope we will.

One of the pleasant gifts of our renewed relationship is an awareness of who is making those strange, distant howls, yips, and barks on warm evenings. The sounds remind us of an earlier, wilder time. We can almost see Señor Coyote silhouetted against a full moon, nose and narrow snout pointed to the heavens, piercing a Berkeley evening with his special calls for friendship. He is a wonderful reminder of the richness of wildlife living in, and on the edge of, urban centers. The carnival is all around us if we take the time to look and enjoy it.

+++

As time goes on, the members of The Animal Carnival change; we miss them one and all when they have gone. But they are never forgotten. Whether it is Grundoone with her grass snakes, Nibs with his mole; Punkin with claws out for a landing; Buffy and the Bear exploring park lanes with us; Spot and Misto enjoying calamari; Toby searching for the perfect tail, with Ms. Holly frightened that he will find it; or Sammy studying attacking jay birds or other forms of wildlife previously unknown to her, each continues to offer us joyful memories and smiles on a regular basis.

The cast of characters of the animal carnival changes, but not the basic elements that make it important—love, companionship, joy, sorrow—and life. These make up the never-ending chain that links the characters we know and have known over the past fifty years.

To our old friends no longer with us, good-bye until we meet again.

To our friends yet to be, welcome to our lives and the carnival. You will bless and enrich them both.

As I write these words a new handsome, young buck, with six points, has come into the garden to take the afternoon sun on the leaf mulch pile.

"Welcome young fellow. Enjoy the day with us."

The carnival continues.

210

Señor Coyote

Handsome young buck

And the bell ringers still come

ROBERT L. and FRAN (RUTH) WILLIAMS SMITH are native Californians. Robert's professional career was dedicated to the administration and reform of juvenile and criminal justice at the local, state, and federal levels. Fran worked with programs serving children with learning and developmental disabilities while also pursuing photography, her hobby. They continue to make their home in Berkeley, California with their many domestic and wild animal friends.